Welcome to W9-AQV-461

THE

EVERYTHING

PARENT'S GUIDES ®

AS A PARENT, you're swamped with conflicting advice and parenting techniques that tell you what is best for your child. THE EVERYTHING® PARENT'S GUIDES get right to the point about specific issues. They give you the most recent, up-to-date information on parenting trends, behavior issues, and health concerns—providing you with a detailed resource to help you ease your parenting anxieties.

THE EVERYTHING® PARENT'S GUIDES are an extension of the bestselling *Everything*® series in the parenting category. These family-friendly books are designed to be a one-stop guide for parents. If you want authoritative information on specific topics not fully covered in other books, THE EVERYTHING® PARENT'S GUIDES are the perfect resource to ensure that you raise a healthy, confident child.

Visit the entire Everything® series at everything.com

THE EVERYTHING®

PARENT'S GUIDES

Raising a Successful Child

Dear Reader,

It is my greatest hope that you will be able to find what you are looking for in *The Everything® Parent's Guide to Raising a Successful Child*. It has been a pleasure, and a learning experience, to write it for you.

When I first became a parent, it wasn't in the normal fashion. I accepted a position at a teen home and was asked to "parent" them. No problem, right? I can't begin to count all of the mistakes I made, even with all of the effective parenting courses I took. But then something happened. I experienced the miracle of birth and had my first daughter. The depth of love and wonder that I gained from having this child, and the two after her, gave me just what I needed to parent. I can now pick and choose from all of the expert advice available using my love for my children as a foundation.

Please use the love you have for your child, as the basis for picking and choosing what advice you will follow. With you in the driver's seat, with a trunk load of resources, and using love as the gas, your child will be a success and so will you.

Denise D. Witmer

THE
EVERYTHING®
PARENT'S GUIDE TO
RAISING A SUCCESSFUL CHILD

All you need to encourage your
child to excel at home and school

Denise D. Witmer

A

Adams Media
Avon, Massachusetts

Publishing Director: Gary M. Krebs
Managing Editor: Kate McBride
Copy Chief: Laura MacLaughlin
Acquisitions Editor: Bethany Brown
Development Editor: Karen Johnson Jacot
Production Editor: Jamie Wielgus

Production Director: Susan Beale
Production Manager: Michelle Roy Kelly
Series Designer: Daria Perreault
Cover Design: Paul Beatrice, Frank Rivera
Layout and Graphics: Colleen Cunningham
Rachael Eiben, Michelle Roy Kelly,
John Paulhus, Daria Perreault, Erin Ring

An Everything® Series Book.
Everything® and everything.com® are registered trademarks of F+W Publications, Inc.

Published by Adams Media, an F+W Publications Company
57 Littlefield Street, Avon, MA 02322 U.S.A.
www.adamsmedia.com

ISBN: 1-59337-043-1
Printed in the United States of America.

J I H G F E D C B A

Library of Congress Cataloging-in-Publication Data
Witmer, Denise D.
The everything parent's guide to raising a successful child/
Denise D. Witmer.
p.   cm.
(An everything series book)
ISBN 1-59337-043-1
1. Parenting. 2. Child rearing. 3. Emotional intelligence.
4. Children–Conduct of life. 5. Success in children. I. Title.
II. Series: Everything series.
HQ755.8.W624   2004
613.9'6–dc22   2003026249

This publication is designed to provide accurate and authoritative information with regard to the subject matter covered. It is sold with the understanding that the publisher is not engaged in rendering legal, accounting, or other professional advice. If legal advice or other expert assistance is required, the services of a competent professional person should be sought.
—From a *Declaration of Principles* jointly adopted by a Committee of the American Bar Association and a Committee of Publishers and Associations

Many of the designations used by manufacturers and sellers to distinguish their products are claimed as trademarks. Where those designations appear in this book and Adams Media was aware of a trademark claim, the designations have been printed with initial capital letters.

Cover photo by Image Source.

This book is available at quantity discounts for bulk purchases.
For information, call 1-800-872-5627.

All the examples and dialogues used in this book are fictional, and have been created by the author to illustrate disciplinary situations.

suc·cess (sək-ses′) ► *n.*
1. The beauty and joy of raising a child to choose the best path for life's ongoing journey, measured not by any standard means but by the realization of how far he or she has come.

Dedication

To my husband, daughters, parents, and the parents before them

• • •

Contents

Introduction

YOUR CHILD IS NOT A LUMP OF CLAY that needs to be molded. He already has a shape and form. He comes with potential. He has natural abilities. Your job as a parent is more like polishing a golden statue. You have to use a soft cloth and the right type of polish in order for his abilities to shine through.

You also are a golden statue. You have potential. You came into parenting with abilities. You'll be polishing parts of your identity as you raise your child. By parenting, you are growing and developing into a new person. Keep this mind when you choose between a piece of sandpaper and a soft cloth. As a family, you all grow together. If you become stagnant as a parent, your child will not be able to grow to his full potential. But, if you are willing to learn new ways of parenting and to apply them, both you and your child will shine. Does that mean everything you try will work? No, not everything, possibly even most things may not work. Because your family is unique, you'll need to test things out, and you will still make mistakes even though you have followed the best parenting advice from the experts.

However, you are not destined to repeat the mistakes of your parents. You are destined to make your own. Isn't that wonderful? When you accepted the job of being a parent, you had no experience and knew you were bound to make mistakes. You may not have wanted to look at it that way, but the mistakes did happen. So, you started the search for information. You did this because you have parenting abilities. You have the potential to parent your child successfully. You just need that ever-elusive parenting manual that everyone tells you doesn't exist. Well, it does. It exists in your heart and mind. It may take a library full of parenting books, magazines, and Web sites for you to discover all of the instructions—and you will need to go back to learn more often—but your parenting manual is available twenty-four hours a day, seven days a week.

Most parents agree that they want their child to be something. They want him to be happy, smart, respectful, honest, responsible, and more. Most children have the ability to be just what their parents want them to be. Now the trick lies in looking up what you want your child to be in your parenting manual, reading what type of cloth and polish you'll need to use, and then use it correctly. But if you rub one area too hard, you'll smudge another. For instance, if you push your child too hard to be smart, he may cheat and tarnish his honesty. All of the parenting resources, cloths, and polish will not help your child become what you want him to be if your parenting manual does not include notes on his individual abilities, strengths, and weaknesses.

Learn first what your child needs and what his abilities are. Then use the strength of the love you feel for him to guide him toward his goal. Use your potential to learn what you'll need to get him there. Fill in your parenting manual by developing the unique skills and tools you'll need to give him the attributes of success.

CHAPTER 1

Where Do Successful Children Come From?

S UCCESSFUL CHILDREN COME from all walks of life. Every background, culture, financial status, or religion produces successful children. Yours can be one of them. You already have the tools you need to help your child be successful . . . you just need to know how best to use them.

Every Child Can Be Successful

The definition of a successful child is *your* child. Everything about the child you have brought into this world defines some degree of success. Even a child who faces a major life crisis is capable of making a success out of his life. Maya Angelou did not have an easy childhood. Read her autobiographical book *I Know Why the Caged Bird Sings*. Yet, she went on to become a famous writer, poet, speaker, civil-rights activist, and a phenomenal woman.

Success is relative; every life has its ups and downs. Your child will continue to have small and large successes throughout her life. It is natural to want to do everything you can to help ensure that she has the best chances at success as she grows up.

Take a Deep Breath—You're Normal

Have you noticed that much of the parenting advice today can tend to make you feel like the worst parent in the world? It's great advice, but many times you'll feel as though you have no clue how to incorporate it into your family's structure. Or you worry so much that it won't work, that you fail to try. Or, worse yet, you don't even go looking for parenting advice because you feel that you are the only one having this problem, and you're embarrassed.

Take a deep breath—you're normal! Every parent experiences these feelings, and every parent can use good advice at one time or another, or all the time for that matter. This is true now, and it has been true throughout history.

 ESSENTIAL

Although very few problems are a crisis, don't overlook a problem your child is having by thinking "kids will be kids." Yes, it is normal for problems to come up, but you should always strive to help your child fix his or her mistakes.

A Look at Parenting in the 1800s

In parenting, not all that much has changed. Take a look at these excerpts from *Advice to a Mother on the Management of Her Children*, by Pye Henry. It was published in 1880.

I am not overstating the importance of the subject in hand when I say, that a child is the most valuable treasure in the world, that he is the precious gift of God, that he is the source of a mother's greatest and purest enjoyment, that he is the strongest bond of affection between her and her husband.

A child should be happy; he must, in every way, be made happy; everything ought to be done to conduce to his happiness, to give him joy, gladness, and pleasure. Happy he should be as happy as the day is long. Kindness should be lavished upon him. Make a child understand that you love him; prove it in your actions—these are better than words; look after his little pleasures—join in his little sports; let him never hear a morose word—it would rankle in his breast, take deep root, and in due time bring forth bitter fruit. Love! Let love be his pole-star; let it be the guide and the rule of all you do and all you say unto him.

Pleasant words ought always to be spoken to a child; there must be neither snarling, nor snapping, nor snubbing, nor loud contention toward him. If there be it will ruin his temper and disposition, and will make him hard and harsh, morose and disagreeable . . . Never allow a child to be teased; it spoils his temper. If he be in a cross humour take no notice of it, but divert his attention to some pleasing object. This may be done without spoiling him. Do not combat bad temper with bad temper—noise with noise. Be firm, be kind, be gentle, be loving, speak quietly, smile tenderly, and embrace him fondly, but insist upon implicit obedience, and you will have, with God's blessing, a happy child.

Respiration, digestion, and a proper action of the bowels, imperatively demand fresh air and exercise. Ill health will inevitably ensue if boys and girls are cooped up a great part of the day in a close room. A distinguished writer of the present day says: The children of the very poor are always out and about. In this respect they are an example to those careful mammas who keep their children, the whole day long, in their chairs, reading, writing, ciphering, drawing, practicing music les-sons, doing crotchet work, or anything, in fact, except running about in spite of the sunshine always peeping in and inviting them out of doors; and who, in the due course of time, are surprised to find their children showing up with incurable heart, head, lung, or stomach complaints.

Young minds cannot appreciate great sacrifices made for them; they judge their parents by the words and deeds of every-day life. They are won by little kindnesses, and alienated by little acts of neglect or impatience. One complaint unnoticed, one appeal unheeded, one lawful request arbitrarily refused, will be remembered by your little ones more than a thousand acts of the most devoted affection.

Trends in Parenting, 1890s to the Present

The trend in parenting in the late nineteenth century and throughout the twentieth century looks like a tennis match, going back and forth between two different types of parenting, thereby defining the parenting style of the day. The two types are basically based on who was at the reins of the family: the parent or the child. When the child was at the reins, the type is called "child-centered," and you will tend to see a permissive style of parenting emerge. The permissive style allowed the child to set the pace. When the parent is at the reins, the type is called "parent-centered," and you will see a more restrictive/authoritative style of parenting. In the restrictive style of parenting, the parent set the pace.

In a study of more than eighty years of women's magazines, two different researchers identified these trends in parenting:

- *1890s–1920:* Permissive, child-centered.
- *1920–1935:* Restrictive/Authoritative, parent-centered.
- *1935–1950s:* Permissive, child-centered.
- *1960s–1980s:* Restrictive/Authoritative, firm but loving, centered on both parent and child.
- *1990s–present:* Restrictive/Authoritative, firm but loving, centered on both parent and child; return of spanking debate; fear of breakdown of family.

Your Individualism Is the Key

Who are you? Do you remember? Parents tend to start to define themselves as a parent. *I'm a mother with three daughters.* But remember, that *isn't* who you are. It is part of a job you've taken and will influence who you become, but it isn't your sole identity.

Take a good look in the mirror and say who you are. Take a deep breath. Start with your name and then ask yourself:

- What are my likes and dislikes?
- Where have I come from and where do I want to go?
- When I'm feeling capable, what do I do?
- When I'm feeling incapable, what do I do?

 ALERT!

> Don't step too far away from who you are in order to be who you think you need to be as a parent. You don't have to change to meet someone else's criteria for "good parent." This will cause you inner turmoil and will teach your child that who he is isn't good enough either. Your individualism is the key. Who you are will help your child become the success you want him to be.

Using Your Individual Skills

Do you know what your abilities are? Your individual parenting skills will be based on them. For instance, if you have a superior memory, you'll feel comfortable when your children's schedule gets a little hectic. If not, you will want to invest in a personal planner. In other words, you'll form parenting skills that enhance the abilities you have and compensate for the abilities you do not have. Therefore, they become your unique individual parenting skills.

Generally, you will be able to see what abilities you have and what skills you need as you need them. This means that as a parent you will need to fall back and regroup often. For example, when your child starts school, you will see that organization is a must, not only daily, but seasonally. You know you need to bring a jacket to work with you on a fall morning because the day can start out brisk and become quite warm by afternoon. You will learn to be organized in a similar manner for your child. You've spent all of your life thinking ahead for yourself. Now you have to take those organizational skills, turn them into *parenting* organizational skills, and start thinking ahead for your child. Of course you will learn this by trial and error; therefore your child may be a little chilly one day. That's okay. Your parenting skills will always be in constant development.

Once you start to develop your parenting skills, you'll need to put them to use, probably often. Every minute of every day is not unlikely. This may sound like a lot of work, and it is—but it isn't. You will learn that as a parent using your skills brings rewards like proud moments, hugs and kisses, and so much more. The work part of parenting is worth it.

 ESSENTIAL

You need to be comfortable with your abilities. You don't have to be perfect; so don't hold on to any guilt if you are not capable of a certain task. Improvise and learn a skill that will compensate for it.

Shape a Healthy Family Dynamic

Family dynamics refers to how family members relate to and interact with one another. With more and more children in the United States being raised and cared for by people other than their biological parents, the concept of "family" is constantly evolving and expanding. In addition, many families today, regardless of household arrangement, find themselves faced with special circumstances. In every case the caregiver can shape the attributes for success in children by using their skills to create functional parenting tools.

The Two-Parent Family

The two-parent family is the traditional family structure. Although it comes with the benefit of not having any added baggage, it does have its difficulties. Decisions need to be made when you parent a child. The question then is, who makes the decisions? The answer to this question can weaken or strengthen this family dynamic. As a unique individual, your opinions will differ from your spouse's opinions. The spanking debate can be used as an example. If you do not feel that spanking is an appropriate form of discipline, yet your spouse does, you will need to resolve that issue before discipline is ever needed. If you do not resolve this issue, you or your spouse will feel resentment every time you need to discipline. That resentment will build and weaken your family structure.

The relationship between the two parents can also be either a strength or a weakness to this family structure. All marriages have their ups and downs. Your children will be directly affected by these ups and downs. It is advantageous for the two-parent family to always keep this in mind. When you have a conflict, fight fairly and do so away from your children.

The best way to handle an argument with your spouse is to prevent it entirely. Keep the lines of communication open, find time daily for each other, and remember that you and your spouse will grow and change. If a conflict still arises, fight fairly—you owe it to yourself, your spouse, and your child. Don't bring up any history and try to stay on topic so that you can resolve the issue at hand. When the conflict is resolved, say you're sorry and forgive your partner. Then do something together that you will both enjoy.

The Single-Parent Family

Single-parent families face a multitude of problems, but none that can't be handled. Often, the main problem is not enough time to do double the work. When there isn't a partner to share the load, life becomes even more hectic. There are more financial worries, there is less time to enjoy your child, and there is the hectic schedule of keeping a household organized. Single parents can and do compensate by living frugally and keeping as organized as possible. They lean on family and friends to help with the little things, like car-pooling for their child while they are at work, and they make it a point to make the time for their child.

Depending on the circumstances, you may face some obstacles to turning a single-parent situation into a healthy family dynamic for your child. If you are widowed, for instance, you will need to work through your grief and help your child work through hers also. If you are divorced, you will need to work with your ex-spouse in order to form a stable parenting unit that works for your child.

 ALERT!

Children who grow up in single-parent homes often have problems building trusting and loving relationships with a significant other because they have not been exposed to it. If you're a single parent, expose your child to these relationships through family and friends.

Grandparents Raising Grandchildren

Believe it or not, according to the AARP, there are eight times more children in grandparent-headed homes than in the foster care system. Grandparents are responding to a problem in the middle generation, such as death of the parent, illness, divorce, immaturity, incarceration of the parent, parental substance abuse, child abuse, or neglect. They are motivated by the love they feel for their grandchildren, and they step in to fill a gap created by the problem.

Grandparents who are heading the family face special problems. They must investigate and resolve legal questions about custody, guardianship, or adoption. Without legal status, grandparents may not be able to enroll their grandchildren in school or make medical decisions for them.

Parenting the Adopted Child

Often forming a healthy family dynamic with an adopted child involves the decision whether to tell the child he is adopted. Some parents prefer to wait until the child is older, believing he will understand better. Others believe that a child should never remember a time when he didn't know about his adoption.

 **FACT**

> Regardless of the route that your family chooses on when and how, it is important to remember that a child should not be told once about her adoption but talked with throughout each of the stages of childhood development. The key is to provide a comfortable, accepting atmosphere in which a child can communicate the questions she is thinking about and get the answers she is searching for.

Forming Attributes for Success

You cannot parent on your abilities alone. You need to use them to form skills that are based on the unique needs of family. You need to take these skills and develop parenting tools that you can pull out when needed. And you need to set parenting goals. These goals are the attributes you want to instill in your child—the attributes that will lead them to a successful life.

So what are your goals for your child? You want him to be honest and fair; therefore, you want him to have good character. You want him to be intelligent; therefore, you want him to have a willingness to learn. You want him to be able to face the challenges his life will bring him; therefore, you want him to be resilient. You want him to like himself and know who he is on the inside; therefore, you want him to have high self-esteem. You want him to find the happiness and joy you have found in your family; therefore, you want him to have the ability to love. Once you have your goals, start drawing the map of their achievement. It will take a lifetime to finish, as you will be parenting your child for the rest of your life.

Today's Family Life

Today's definition of family life can be summed up in one word—hectic! The responsibility of a family involves using all of your time and effort. Even the most organized person will still have a hard time trying to schedule in everything a family needs to do. It can be hard to find time to handle all your family responsibilities, and even harder to find time for family fun. But remember that with children, love is attention and time. You need to make time to give them the attention they need, even if that means giving up a personal goal.

It falls to the parent to make time for the family. You may need to change your schedule to suit your family's needs. It will also fall to you to reinforce the idea to your children that having family time is important.

CHAPTER 2

"Successful" versus "Picture Perfect"

W HEN YOU GET YOUR FAMILY TOGETHER to take a family picture, you spend quite a bit of time getting it all ready. You have to schedule haircuts, buy new outfits, get a sitting time that doesn't interfere with the baby's nap, and so on. In the end, it is all worth it—you have a perfect picture that you can proudly display in your home. When you look at it, you forget about all the work it took. Success is like that.

Your Picture of a Perfect Family

You probably have a picture of what the perfect family looks like in your head. Children come home from school with smiling faces and do their homework, babies sleep through the night, your teenager's bedroom is spotless, etc. Sounds perfect, doesn't it?

Unfortunately, reality isn't perfect. Your baby is going to be awake in the middle of the night, and he doesn't care that you need to get up early in the morning. Your teenager is going to be late for curfew, probably more than once. You will pace back and forth in your living room imagining all kinds of horrors that could have befallen him until he walks through the door. Then he will ask you why you're so upset. This is the real world of being a parent. Perfect just doesn't belong.

If you find yourself relying on how things "should be" with your family, it's time for you to stop looking at your picture of a perfect family. "Should be" will only cloud your vision. When you start looking at how things really are, red eyes and all—that is when you begin the road to success—for you, for your family, and for your child.

Your Expectations

There are two core types of parental expectations: one to manage behaviors and the other to help a child succeed in his accomplishments. Managing behaviors by setting reasonable expectations will help your child develop character traits such as confidence, responsibility, and self-worth. Helping your child succeed through reasonable expectations will boost her self-esteem and encourage her to reach for even higher goals.

 FACT

While sometimes you will see the phrases *self-worth* and *self-esteem* used interchangeably, they are two different things. Self-worth is a feeling of value simply because you are a living, breathing human being. Self-esteem is the feeling of respect you have for yourself.

It may seem as though you're walking a tightrope at times when you are deciding what you can reasonably expect from your child. Setting expectations too high or too low can lead to undesirable behaviors or underdeveloped accomplishments. The key to setting both types of parental expectations is to keep the balance.

Setting Expectations for Positive Behaviors

Setting reasonable expectations for positive behaviors isn't as hard as you may think. It takes three simple steps: think about what positive behavior you are expecting your child to exhibit, clear communication about those expectations, and take time to develop and carry out your course of action. Oftentimes, parents don't follow through with each of these simple steps. Therefore, the outcome isn't the positive behavior they were seeking from their child.

 ALERT!

You must accept that your children will not meet your expectations all the time. As long as your expectations are reasonable and remain consistent, your child will begin over time to meet them more often than not.

When thinking about the behaviors you would like your child to exhibit, ask yourself these questions:

- Is my child developmentally ready to carry out the behavior?
- Will the behavior result in positive experiences for my child?
- Can I clearly communicate to my child the behavior I am looking for?
- Do I have the time to develop and carry out the course of action?

If you answered yes to these three questions, your expectation is reasonable.

Let's take a two-year-old who is showing interest in potty training as an example. Is she developmentally ready to carry out the behavior? Yes. She is at the right age and she is showing interest. Will the behavior result in positive experiences for her? Yes. She will not have to be uncomfortable in a dirty diaper any longer. Can you clearly communicate to your child the positive behavior you are looking for? Yes. There are many children's books devoted to learning how to use the potty, or you may use one of her friends as an example. Do you have the time to develop and carry out the course of action? You will need to make a conscious decision to adjust your schedule and to show patience and encouragement in order to answer yes to this question.

Setting Expectations for Accomplishments

Since the benefits of setting expectations for accomplishments will often be evident in the future, you may tend to worry about them more. Are you pushing too hard or are you not pushing hard enough? Does your child really have an interest in playing the piano or is he taking the lessons to please you? Many times the answer to these questions will be "I don't know." That's okay! The future is the unknown. Set expectations so that your child enjoys and learns from life's journey. Accomplishments in whatever your child decides to strive for will follow.

 **QUESTION?**

What if my child rebels?
If your child begins to rebel, she is sending you a message and it's time to take a step back. Get more input from her and revise your expectations.

Create an environment that fosters your child's unique strengths. If you set reasonable expectations based on these strengths, it will go a long way toward building self-confidence, which is essential to long-term success. One key in setting expectations so that your child will enjoy and learn during the journey to an accomplishment is to help your child become self-motivated. This is done by:

- Making sure the goal is something your child wants, not just what you want for him.
- Allowing her to have input into how the accomplishment is achieved.
- Helping him assess and refine his own expectations.
- Acknowledging small steps—as well as big ones—toward an accomplishment.

Children Who Set Expectations Too High

Characteristics of a child with a type A personality include demonstrating a strong sense of urgency; having a hard time relaxing or feeling guilty when relaxing; determining to win every game, even when playing with those who are less skilled; doing everything rapidly; exhibiting impatience with the normal pace of events; and tending to evaluate all activities in terms of measurable results.

If your child has a type A personality, you may have to help him learn to lower his expectations. You can do this by breaking down the goal into smaller goals. Encourage him to focus on the smaller goal. As he completes each of the smaller goals, you know he will be accomplishing the larger goal, but don't mention it. Keep him focused on each of the smaller goals by praising each step. This will teach him to slow down and take things step by step.

Children Who Set Expectations Too Low

By nature, children are not lazy. If you find your child avoids activities and setting goals, or has no expectations, you should see your pediatrician and make sure there are no physical problems. Often, something as simple as a mild recurring ear infection can go unnoticed but manifest itself in slothlike behavior.

A child who sets expectations too low may be fearful of the outcome. Encourage your child to set her expectations just a little higher but still at a point that you are sure she will be able to achieve. Compromise. Set your expectations between where she has set them and where you feel they should be. By achieving the compromised expectation, she will gain confidence and will be more likely to raise the bar on her own.

Gender Differences

When boys meet their expectations, they attribute the success to their abilities, which builds their self-confidence. When they fail to meet their expectations, they attribute the failure to external forces, shielding their self-confidence. With girls, it's just the opposite. Therefore, every time a girl fails, she attributes it to lack of ability, and this wears down her self-confidence.

Generally, you'll want to strive to praise girls and boys in the same manner. Not praising individual talents—no matter what they may be—can erode your child's self-confidence, resulting in an underdeveloped talent and keeping him from developing other talents. Or he may set himself against you, fight you all the way, and place you outside his success when he achieves it.

Defining the Successful Child

A successful child is one who uses her abilities to develop ever-increasing skills that help form the positive personal attributes that will lead her to a successful life. A child's individual abilities make her unique. She uses her skills to develop positive experiences. She has a strong sense of self and looks forward to accomplishing goals.

Successful children have parents who are always working on their parenting skills. Their parents use these skills to enhance and encourage their child's abilities. They create useful parenting tools to build the attributes their child needs to succeed.

Successful children become successful adults who have high levels of self-esteem and self-worth. They enjoy learning new things and being with those they love. They have good character, morals, and values. They are happy.

Success means having a favorable outcome or obtaining something that was desired or intended. As we all have individual desires or intentions, we all have different ideas of what a successful life includes. Generally, people define a successful life as being happy, healthy, and able to enjoy life to its fullest.

Your Child's Abilities

Your child's abilities are the things he is capable of doing, not what a book says he should be capable of doing or what you wish he were capable of doing. Do not push your child to do something that he is not capable of doing at all. For instance, a three-year-old child who enjoys scribbling in his coloring book should not be pushed to color within the lines. If you push for neatness, he may begin to ignore coloring altogether. Then he will never enjoy learning to color between the lines.

ALERT!

A child who once enjoyed an activity but all of a sudden no longer wants to participate in it may have had a negative experience that you are unaware of. Talk with your child by asking general questions; then follow up with teachers, coaches, and other parents.

Try this activity to help you focus on your child's abilities. Down the left-hand side of a piece of paper, make a list of your child's abilities, everything that your child does well. Be honest! You can even scale each ability from one to ten—one being "does okay" to ten being "does great." Down the right-hand side of the same piece of paper, make a list of all the activities he likes to do. Cross-check the list, matching up the activities he likes to do with the abilities it takes to do them. You'll find that your child has gravitated toward activities that match his abilities. He has set himself up for success.

As his parent, you can help him increase his chances of success simply by making those activities that match his abilities available to him. As your child experiences more through these activities, he will be fine-tuning his abilities. This will, in turn, lead to even more success.

Your Child's Ever-Increasing Skills

A child who has the ability to run quickly may go out for a sport such as soccer where that ability is useful. There, she will learn to dribble a ball with her feet. Through practice she will begin to be able to run quickly while dribbling the ball. As long as her experiences with soccer remain positive, she will continue to improve her soccer skills.

Forming Positive Personal Attributes

Personal attributes are those qualities that make your child who he is. Is he active? Is he organized? Does he like to learn? These qualities are very much like the ones you would list on your resume.

Although your child is predisposed to his attributes, they can be formed and reformed. A disorganized child can be taught skills that will help him become organized. A child who dislikes reading can be taught better reading skills and given material she finds interesting so that she will learn to like to read. A child who tends to run late can be taught better organizational skills that will help him be prompt.

Your Family Goals

Family goals will help your family keep a clear vision of what is truly important in life. They will help you stay focused on each other when life gets busy. They will give a sense of belonging and a positive outlook for the future. To set family goals, create a "family mission statement." The mission statement is a plan that includes your family's goals and beliefs. It has realistic expectations that set the family up for success.

Creating a Family Mission Statement

The most important part of the family mission statement is that all members of the family participate in making it. If any person in the family is not a part of developing the statement, he or she will feel left out of the family circle. Therefore, the main goal of having a strong sense of belonging will not be accomplished. It is imperative to get input from the oldest to the youngest. If your parent lives with you, he or she needs to be included as well.

Start by having a family meeting. Ask everyone: What do you want most for this family? Write down all of the answers and develop a vision statement. The vision statement is the first part of your family's mission statement. It is your family's long-term goal. It may read something like this: "We desire a loving family where family members are happy and supported." Read the vision statement out loud and make sure everyone agrees with the wording. Next ask: How should we try to accomplish our vision? Write down all the answers. These are the behaviors that are important to your family. They include family rules, how members of the family would like to be treated, and things that are important to each person.

 ESSENTIAL

Do not use the family mission statement as a behavioral modification tool. If you use it constantly to remind your children about their behavior, it will break down the ultimate goal of the tool, which is to develop a strong sense of belonging.

The last part of your family mission statement will be the short-term goals your family would like to accomplish. These goals are set to help you accomplish your family vision. They can be as simple as having dessert with the meal every Wednesday night. These goals should be realistic, positive, and measurable, and have a specific time frame attached to them. For example, if you would like to spend more time together as a family, schedule a family game night each week. You would write on your family mission statement: "In order to spend more time together, the Jones family will play games at 7 P.M. every Thursday evening."

Place this statement in a predominant spot in your home where everyone will see it and read it often. A good spot might be on the front of the refrigerator. At family meetings, refer to the statement to assess how well you are working at achieving your family goals. Reassess the statement as time goes on and your children grow.

Learning How to Auto-Focus

When you want to take a picture, you probably put your camera on auto-focus. You decide what the focal point will be so that your picture doesn't come out fuzzy or blurred. The camera will then focus on the most important part of your picture and make it come out the clearest.

As you look at your family with a realistic eye, set up reasonable expectations, remember that success is based on the individual, and start feeling a sense of belonging as a family, you will begin learning how to auto-focus on the important aspects of your child's life. You'll see the wonders of his artwork, instead of all the paint he got on the floor. When you do, take a step back and recognize your accomplishment.

Turn Your Picture into a Video

Videos are wonderful. They capture actions and can be edited. You can rewind and repeat them as many times as you wish. Although you'll always get the same outcome, you may be able to pick up on a few more aspects every time you watch it.

Successful families are like videos. They are never still long enough for anyone to take the perfect picture. Their dynamics change as they grow, and there is always a lot of action. They auto-focus on the important parts of life's journey and edit out the mistakes. Start shooting your own video. Don't just clip a perfect picture here and there. Enjoy the action!

CHAPTER 3

Parenting Strengths and Weaknesses

Y OUR STRENGTHS AND WEAKNESSES are a part of you. By assessing what they are, building on your strengths, and accepting your weaknesses, you can gain the confidence it takes to use the five key skills of parenting. That is your first step to helping your child be a success.

Your Individualism Is a Strength

You are an individual, with your own traits that set you apart from anyone else. You have your own style and attributes. You bring with you into your family your own uniqueness. It is yours and yours alone. It is called your individualism. Each individual brings something different into the family. This is what helps mold and define your family, making your family distinct from other families. This gives you a sense of belonging. You belong with a distinct set of people, your family, which your individualism helps define. That is why your individualism is a strength.

Celebrating Your Child's Individualism

You'll hear about your child's physical attributes and temperament every time you visit relatives. She has

daddy's eyes, she has her mother's smile, she has her grandfather's nose, or she has her grandmother's sweet temperament. All these things add up to your child—an individual who is the composite of you and all of your family before you.

 **FACT**

Specific genes determine hereditary traits. Children carry two genes for each trait, one from the mother's egg and one from the father's sperm. Your child's looks and temperament will depend on which genes she receives and which are dominant or recessive (suppressed).

Praising Your Children Individually

When you have more than one child, you can get caught up in what one can do well, and the others don't do as well. Parents tend to compare and contrast their children without even noticing it. When you do this, you not only bring down the self-esteem of the child who isn't wonderful at that certain task, but you also boost one child above the other.

Although it is normal for others to compare family members, you need to be aware, as a parent, that your opinion means so much more to your children. When you say to your second son that you wish he would get into a sport like his older brother, you are telling him that you haven't taken notice of what his talents are, what he is good at, or what he might want to do. It is an easy trap to fall into, which is why you'll hear parents do it all the time.

Instead of grouping your children together, recognize their individual likes and dislikes. When your child is searching for something to be good at, focus on her likes and offer choices as opposed to asking her to try something one of her siblings is good at. When each child finds her niche, she will be able to focus on her individuality and build her identity. Other people (including you) won't think of her as just someone's sister. Her self-esteem will rise accordingly.

When you help each child find his own niche and support him in it, you will be better able to praise him individually. You will be able to communicate that you like each child best, that you truly like him as a person. This is really important as your children get older and assert their own personalities. Your child knows that you love him, but he may often wonder if you like him. Praising him for what he is good at without comparing him to his siblings will show him that you do indeed like him.

 ESSENTIAL

> Praising children works when you praise them for something they value. Your child will not value being praised for being good at or almost as good at something her sibling does. Praise your child's uniqueness to boost her self-esteem.

Save the Memories

Your child is only going to take his first step once, he is only going to his first day of kindergarten once, and he is only going to get his driver's permit once—you need to save these memories for him. It doesn't have to be an elaborate scrapbook. It can be notes jotted down on a calendar, or anything that keeps a record of his childhood. He will cherish it and share it with his own children. Therefore, make sure you get a picture of him in the most outrageous fad outfit of his time. This will be something you and your grandchildren will have a good laugh over.

Where Are Your Parenting Strengths and Weaknesses?

What are your personal strengths and weaknesses as a parent? Have you ever taken the time to assess yourself? We all bring certain qualities to any situation we face. Sometimes those qualities are beneficial and work well with the situation, and sometimes those qualities work against the situation. Sometimes a quality that is normally beneficial can turn into one that works against a situation when you have children. Take punctuality, for instance. If you like to be on time as much as possible, you may begin to have problems when you have children because, through no fault of their own, children can make you late. For example, babies spit up, normally after you're ready for work and walking out the door. This can cause you stress if you like to be on time, making punctuality a strength that works against you in that situation by causing you additional stress and worry.

Take a look at these personal strengths and weaknesses and assess where you are on a scale of one to ten, with one meaning that you do not have the trait at all and ten meaning that you have the trait to the point of excess. Think of situations in which your strengths may have been weaknesses when it came to raising your child.

Active	Flexible
Astute	Honest
Broad-minded	Intuitive
Compatible	Logical
Conscientious	Loyal
Consistent	Methodical
Courteous	Persistent
Dependable	Productive
Determined	Proficient
Diligent	Resourceful
Disciplined	Self-reliant
Effective	Sincere
Energetic	Straightforward
Enthusiastic	Talented
Fair	Thoughtful

Honestly assessing which areas are your strengths will help give you insight into how you handle situations with your child. If you are competitive, you may have a hard time losing at checkers to your eight-year-old. Or if you are a disciplined person, you may have a hard time with the hectic schedule of a preteen. No matter what assets you have, your children will make you look at them in a different light.

Your children will also magnify your weaknesses exponentially. Murphy's Law never fails here. If you are a clutter bug, prepare not to be able to find your living room. If you have a quick temper, it will soon be able to be set off in two seconds flat, on the hour, every hour. Another funny thing you will find about your weaknesses is that many times they will also be your child's weaknesses. They will be the things that bother you most about what your child does. The reason it bothers you so much is that you see yourself mirrored in your child. Since, as a parent, you don't want your child to mimic your faults, these will be the things that bother you most.

 ALERT!

Don't let other people determine what your traits are or what they aren't. When someone labels you with a trait, you may begin to act that way because of the label he or she has given you. Don't give others this much power over how you act.

Never feel boxed in by assessing your traits or typing yourself. If you are doing an honest personal assessment, your type merely identifies your preferred way of dealing with the external world. It should give you confidence in your strengths and throw up red flags to help you deal with your weaknesses. It's your free will to use your strengths and work on your weaknesses. That is part of what makes you an individual.

Building Your Family's Strengths

Your family is a combination of all the individuals who define it. It has a life of its own. It is a tangible entity that has its own strengths and weaknesses. There are things in life that affect the entire family as a whole. Lack of time together, lack of money, and personal trauma can cause tension and weaken family bonds.

Strong families have common qualities that promote their strengths. First, they are committed to each other. They give each other support and encouragement through the bad times, and they share in the joy and excitement of the good times. Second, they openly show caring and appreciation for each other. They notice when one member of the family achieves something or needs support. Third, they communicate with each other. When there is a problem or tension among family members, they know how to communicate the problem without hurting anyone's self-esteem. Fourth, they have strong ties with their community. They are involved in community organizations, churches, and schools. They use these ties to strengthen their inner bonds with each other. Fifth, they aren't afraid to seek outside help. If there is a problem they can't handle, they will turn to where they can find the answer.

Strong families are successful families. There is a give-and-take between the individual and the family that strengthens each other. When the individual needs help, the family is there for him. When the family needs help, the individuals support it and strengthen it.

Dos and Don'ts of Strengths and Weaknesses

Here is a quick list of what to remember when you are using your strengths and working out your weaknesses.

- Do give yourself opportunities to encourage your abilities.
- Don't allow one of your abilities to overshadow your other abilities.
- Do develop habits that will strengthen your weaknesses.
- Don't attack yourself because of your weaknesses—everyone has them.

- Do accept criticism graciously.
- Don't give criticism freely.
- Do step out of your comfort zone in order to gain some personal growth.
- Don't overcompensate for your weaknesses—find some level ground.
- Do be aware of others and their priorities.
- Don't dismiss other people because you don't agree with their principles.

Accepting Your Weaknesses

No one is perfect—not many profess to be, but not too many are willing to admit their weaknesses. Parents, like most people, have a hard time acknowledging that some of their actions are weaknesses. When your child spills an entire cup of coffee on your computer and you yell, that is a weakness. It's loss of control and giving in to the impulse to let out your frustration. But, because your frustration is understandable and most parents would have reacted the same way, you don't acknowledge it as a weakness.

There are going to be more times than you want to count when you let yourself be overcome by one of your weaknesses. You'll need to accept that it happens. Many times, it is understandable. But you should still acknowledge it as a weakness and find ways to avoid letting it happening again.

 **FACT**

Psychologist Carl Jung said, "Wisdom accepts that all things have two sides." Your weaknesses can be balanced out by your strengths and may therefore make you stronger. Face your weaknesses, dissect them, and see where they help you in your life.

Suppose, for example, one of your weaknesses is a poor memory. Try as you might to remember when you need to do something or go somewhere, you are constantly forgetting to do it. How can you help yourself in this situation? You could develop a habit of writing things down. By learning always to write everything down and by organizing your time, you will compensate for being forgetful.

There is a good habit for every weakness. By employing the habit, you will compensate for the weakness and become more successful in that area. The habit may even turn your weakness into what others consider a strength.

If you can force yourself to do an action for thirty days straight, you are capable of developing a habit. Your brain will actually grow a "habit node." Try it! Do a simple task for thirty days straight and see how uncomfortable you feel on the thirty-first day if you don't do the task.

Using Your Strengths

After you recognize what your strengths are as a person, you can adapt them to your parenting and create a parenting style of your own. It will be yours, based on your individualism. It will be molded through time by your children's personality. What it won't be is something you've read out of a book. There are four different broad parenting styles, but only one that you should use as the foundation for your unique style.

 ALERT!

Most parents have a definition of what a "good" parent is and what a "bad" parent is. However, you should never be too quick to judge another family. Always remember that you haven't walked a mile in their shoes.

Parenting Styles Not to Emulate

The first parenting style you do not want to emulate is the indifferent style. The indifferent style is basically no parenting style at all. It is the uncaring parent who does nothing for his or her children. The parent lacks emotional involvement, and therefore the children tend to be unsupervised and unloved. You will need to be on the lookout for this type of parent. Your child's friends may be dealing with this style of parenting in their lives. While that is no reason not to allow a friendship, it is something you should keep watch on.

The second style is the authoritarian parenting style. The authoritarian parent believes in setting rules and limits; however, these limitations are more important than showing love or outward affection. They basically believe they are doing their job as parents if they are strict and unbending. They love their children by demanding obedience and respect. They have a hard time being empathetic and listening to their child's side of things. In this style, parents have all of the power and children have no say.

The third style is the permissive parenting style. The permissive parent is the polar opposite of the authoritarian parent. They are very good at being empathetic, but they have problems setting rules and limits. They parent by negotiation, and their children comply because of the relationship they have with their parents. In this style, children have all of the power and there is no respect for limits or rules.

The Parenting Style to Strive For

The fourth style is the balanced parenting style. This style of parent balances both the permissive and authoritarian styles. Parents are the leaders who enforce limits and rules with respect to each individual in the family. There is encouragement, cooperation, and love.

This style is obviously the one that parents should strive for. It is also imperative that you add your individualism to this style. There will be times when you feel the need to let your child take the lead and assert some of his own independence. When you do, you will be leaning toward a more permissive style, and that's okay! For instance, you are a thoughtful person who parents in the balanced style. Your teenage daughter's friend calls five minutes before bedtime because her dog has died and she needs someone to lean on. Your thoughtfulness (individual quality) is going to allow your child to stay up past her bedtime limit for that evening. That is a good thing, because life is never set in stone.

Five Key Skills

There are five key skills that parents need in order to create parenting tools for their toolbox. Once you have a handle on your strengths and weaknesses, and have taken a good look at your parenting style, you are ready to develop these skills. When you develop and use them in your parenting, you will be encouraging your child to develop and use them in her life.

 **FACT**

You won't find the job of parenting listed in the *Occupational Outlook Handbook*. It is not a job for which you are required to have a certain skill level to begin. It is, however, the hardest job you will ever have to do.

Decision-Making

The need to make decisions multiplies exponentially when you have children because there are many more decisions to make. Although you make decisions daily, you may not be going through the process that it takes to make good decisions. When you become a parent, you agonize over the decisions you are making for your child. Will you make the "right" decisions about what you allow him to do or what school he will attend? You can get yourself all tied up in knots with worry.

There is a process to making decisions. When you learn it and use it often, it becomes a great parenting skill. It will give you confidence that you and your family are moving in the right direction toward success. This process is covered in more detail in Chapter 4.

Organizational Skills

Do you plan on having a job while you are raising your children? Does your spouse? How about a social life? Do you want your children to have a social life? What about school? Do you want to know what they are doing in school? And don't forget balanced meals. It would take the brain capacity of Albert Einstein to organize a family on the fly. Even then there would be too much stress to do it well. You need organizational skills when you are a parent. You need to develop them so that your stress levels can stay balanced and you can give your child what she needs—a calm you. Chapter 5 covers this in more detail.

Emotional Intelligence

There are several forms of intelligence that experts have only recently begun to study and understand how they work in everyday life. One of these, emotional intelligence, is being touted as the most important, even more important than intellect or IQ, which is what our school systems base their curricula on. Learning what your emotional intelligence is, and thereby being able to increase it, is a valuable parenting skill. Emotional intelligence is covered further in Chapter 7.

Self-Control and Self-Discipline

No one knows the limits of self-control until they are faced with a two-year-old for twenty-four hours a day, 365 days. For a parent, this skill cannot be more important. Not only do you have to deal with your two-year-old (three-year-old, four-year-old, etc.) and keep your sanity, you also have to do so in a way that sustains their self-esteem. This skill takes practice, and you will need to tweak and practice it more as your child goes through different developmental stages. Chapter 8 covers these further.

Morals and Values

Many people see morals and values as attributes, and they are. But parents are able to take their morals and values and use them as parenting skills. For instance, simply being true to your morals and values is a skill. If you are a religious person, being true to that value would mean finding time to become part of your church community, sharing your beliefs with your child, and remaining true to your faith. Morals and values are covered in more detail in Chapter 9.

CHAPTER 4

Decision-Making

I T'S IMPORTANT to keep in mind that as our children grow older, we will slowly be turning over all of the decision-making to them. We will go from virtually making all of the decisions for an infant to debuting a young adult who is capable of making her own decisions. By gradually turning over the power of decision-making throughout childhood, you will slowly teach your child this key skill to success.

Who Decides?

Children need the stability of knowing who makes the decisions that affect them. Giving them this stability allows them to feel more secure. Security is the basis for trust—not just trust in you the parent but trust in themselves and in the world around them. Therefore, they need someone who makes the decisions, as in the case of an infant or small child, or guides them and approves of their decision, for a child who is growing older. You need to provide this security for them.

As with all key skills, this will require most parents to do some thinking and planning. It will require you to take a look at your family structure and figure out a road map of who makes the decisions. Since families come in all shapes and sizes, we will take a look at two different family structures.

A Two-Parent Home

Does your child come to you or to your partner for an answer? Does he feel you are the decision-maker for important decisions or does he feel it's your spouse? Does he choose to come to you when he wants a "yes" or when he wants an honest answer? Has he gone to one of you, gotten an answer he didn't like, and then proceeded to go to the other with the same question?

Remember, we all have our strengths and weaknesses. Discuss these questions with your partner. Agree to establish a united front when it comes to making decisions. If your child should ask for something and you are unsure, it's okay to take some time to discuss it with your spouse. If your child pressures you to give him an answer immediately, then your answer should be no. While he may miss an opportunity, his inner security is more important. To a child, "no" means "I care enough about you to keep you from doing something that may harm you." Although that will not be your child's immediate response, he will feel a sense of security. A parental unit with a united front offers the most security to a child.

A Single-Parent Home

At first glance it may seem that making decisions in a single-family home is easier than in a two-parent home: however, it is actually often more complex. If there is only one parent, your child always knows who to turn to when she needs an answer. But, being the sole decision-maker can add stress, which will be communicated to your child, either verbally or nonverbally.

If you are co-parenting, it is important to have healthy communication with your former spouse as soon as possible where your children are concerned. Children do not see parents as totally separate entities; they see them as more of a parental unit. When parents divorce, they force their children to redefine their thoughts of the parental unit, causing tension and stress. Working together on decisions that affect your children will help relieve some of the stress for them, even if it seems difficult for you to do at first. It is worth it for your children.

Sometimes it is not possible to have a healthy relationship with your former spouse. Unfortunately, there are people who will use their relationship with their children to hurt their former spouse, and yet you still need to co-parent. If this is the case, do not play into the situation. Do your best to make the decisions that need to be made. Support your child and do your best to put your feelings for your former spouse aside.

If you find that the stress or frustration of handling a former spouse is getting in the way of making decisions for your child, seek out a support group or counselor.

 **FACT**

> According to the 1997 U.S. Census brief, *Children with Single Parents—How They Fare,* of children living with one parent, 38 percent lived with a divorced parent, 35 percent with a never-married parent, 19 percent with a separated parent, 4 percent with a widowed parent, and 4 percent with a parent whose spouse lived elsewhere because of business or some other reason.

Sharing the Responsibility of Decision-Making

Good news! Parents do not have to take on the full responsibility of making decisions for their children. You will get to delegate much of that responsibility over time to someone who feels just as strongly, if not more strongly, about the decisions that need to be made as you do. Who, you ask? Your child!

Even young children should be encouraged to make decisions for themselves. When you guide them through the steps of making decisions, you are helping them build a sense of security in their abilities. A sense of security is a prerequisite to positive self-esteem. Children need this sense of security before they can evaluate their situation realistically or risk the possibility of failure on their own.

ESSENTIAL

Self-esteem is the value we place on what we believe to be true about ourselves. People with high self-esteem consider themselves worthy and view themselves as equal to others. They do not pretend to be perfect; they recognize their limitations and expect to grow and improve.

Steps to Successful Decision-Making

There are several steps to successful decision-making. Help your child take each step one at a time.

1. Realize that a decision needs to be made.
2. Collect information to help make the decision.
3. Identify all of the choices.
4. Examine all of the consequences for each choice.
5. Make the decision.

Praise your child when he starts to show decision-making skills. Begin by praising each step as you guide your child through. Give a little extra praise as he figures out the steps to take on his own. It's okay if he is able to make one decision and not another. Decision-making takes practice, so continue to guide and praise.

Offering Choices

You can help your child learn to make all kinds of decisions by offering her choices often. Practice makes perfect. For instance, instead of laying out your child's clothes for school, say something like: "Your puppy sweater and your blue sweater go with these pants. Which would you like to wear?" This is a clear and specific choice, not one with too many variables. Often that is where parents stumble when allowing children to make choices. If the choice is her entire closet, she will pull out her favorite short set and not care that it is mid-January. This causes quite a bit of frustration for parents and children. Clear and specific choices will help her understand that there are limits to every decision.

When you offer choices to children, they learn successful decision-making skills. They learn that there is a consequence to every decision, that some decisions can be changed and some can't, and that it is okay to make the wrong choice, but you have to go back and try to fix it. They learn how to trust themselves when faced with a problem.

It is a good idea to offer choices to children when the choices are real and the options are acceptable. For instance, suppose your five-year-old daughter wants an ice cream sundae for lunch. This option is only acceptable when you are having a "backward meal." Offer her other choices but make sure they are real. Check to see if you have bread in the cupboard before you offer a sandwich as a choice. This is important because when you make a verbal agreement with your child, she sees it as binding. If you offer a sandwich but then discover that you are out of bread, she is not as likely to trust the choices you offer in the next decision.

 **FACT**

A backward meal is an extremely fun family activity. You serve dessert first, and then the meal. Filling desserts are recommended and don't fuss too much with the meal. For added pleasure, don't clue the family in until they have their dessert in front of them.

There will be times when there is no choice, such as in matters of safety. If your eight-year-old wants to ride his bike, he must wear a helmet. You will have to remain firm on safety issues. Let him know that his choice is to ride his bike with the helmet or to put the bike away.

Communicating Decisions

There are two types of parental tones parents need to use when communicating decisions. One tone is when you have to make a decision for your child, mostly because of safety issues. The second tone is when you are guiding her to make a decision. The way you offer choices to your child can be just as important as the choices you offer.

A parental tone is never a raised voice. When you are angry, use a tone that demonstrates you are serious and you are being firm. If you practice this tone when you are slightly frustrated, it will become easier to use when you are angry.

 ESSENTIAL

Frustration reducing tip: Once you make a decision, do not communicate it to your child until you are able to follow through with it immediately. Even a few minutes can be hard for a small child to wait. If there is going to be lag time, communicate that when you inform him of your decision.

A calm firm tone is needed when you have to communicate a decision that you have made. If your three-year-old is tired and crying, it is not time to offer choices. Asking her if she wants to take a nap or stop crying may stop the crying for a few minutes, but it isn't going to build trust between you and your child. It will not help build her self-confidence, which is what you are trying to achieve when you teach decision-making skills. It will only lead to more frustration. You must decide it is time to take a nap and follow through. In a calm, loving, but firm manner, let your child know that it is time for a nap, and then follow through with your nap routine.

When Good Decisions Go Bad

Unless you have a crystal ball and use it frequently, you've had good decisions go bad. In other words, something came up that you couldn't foresee when you made the decision, and it changed the consequences of the decision and you were not prepared for it. It happens. You know how to fall back, regroup, and do some creative thinking in order to make more decisions that will either change the outcome or make those consequences more livable. Your child doesn't.

When a good decision your child has made goes bad, it can be devastating to her. She may not be developmentally ready to deal with the concept that "life happens." First, console her. Then as soon as possible, help her step back, think creatively, and make the outcome livable. It may be worthwhile to guide her into situations in which she needs to make a few easier decisions so she can build her confidence back up.

When Bad Decisions Go Really Bad

As our children get older, around the age of eleven, they will want to make more and more decisions and ask for less and less of your input. They will do this as they strive for their independence. This age group is known for its impulsivity and may seem to forget all of the decision-making skills that they previously learned. Therefore, they often make bad decisions. These decisions will have consequences that will frustrate and may even frighten you.

When your child makes a bad decision and things go from bad to worse, it is important to let him know that he made a bad decision in a calm but firm manner—once. Then let it go. Help him deal with the consequences, regroup, or whatever needs to be done. Do not nag him about his bad decision. You do not want him to feel shame; it will only hinder his self-worth and self-esteem. He has future decisions to make and you want him to feel capable, not fearful, of making them.

Guilt and shame are feelings often associated with bad decisions. Simply put, guilt is about actions; shame is about the self. Children feel guilt when they do something that goes against their values. It is a signal to either stop the behavior or to re-evaluate the value. Children feel shame when they believe that it is their self that is bad. Children who feel shame basically believe they are unworthy and unlovable. Shame is a primary emotion that calls up brief, intense painful feelings and a sense of inadequacy. Shame brings forth beliefs of "I am a failure." Feelings of shame cause children to shut down so that they can distance from this painful internal state.

 ALERT!

This is often the time that teenagers begin to experiment with smoking, drugs, or alcohol. It is your responsibility as a parent to check up on them, know where they are, and whom they are with. Those things are not within their choices. You must set limits for them.

On the other hand, guilt is something you need to allow your children to feel from time to time. Without it, they may never realize they are doing something wrong or that they need to adjust the standards they have placed on themselves. But shame should be avoided. To say that shame damages the self-esteem is putting it mildly. Shame can literally strip your child of her self-worth.

The Stress of Making Numerous Decisions

Contrary to popular belief, a parent is not capable of making twenty decisions in ten seconds flat. Unfortunately, your child may never seem to be able to recognize this fact. Many parents of children of every age have to deal with this problem, even those with adult children. When we get stressed, we tend to make poor decisions. So, if you're feeling tugged in too many directions, it's important to take a step back. Give yourself the permission to not make any decisions. Tell your child you will take some time to think about it.

Modeling Decision-Making Skills

By modeling successful decision-making skills, you will teach your child to be a creative thinker and problem solver. Over time she will begin to build her self-confidence and trust in her ability to make decisions. In the same light, you need to trust in your parental ability and believe that she is capable of making decisions. Remember as parents, you are slowly working yourselves out of a job.

Birth to Age Two

As you get to know your infant, you will begin to see him express certain preferences. Does he prefer being in your right arm or your left arm? Does he like to sleep on his side or on his back? While an infant can't verbally communicate his choices to you, he will let you know his preferences. He's already begun making decisions based on his basic needs.

As he gets older, offer him this-or-that choices. Verbalize everything! Does he want to play with the blocks or the balls? Does he want the red ball or the green ball?

Ages Three to Five

Children in this age group still need you to spell out that they need to make a decision, what their choices are, and what the consequences of those choices will be. They are capable of making choices on their own once you have set the limits. Structure the choices you offer wisely. The world is a place of endless possibilities to this age group. You will get to experience this firsthand as your child begins to dress herself. A smart parent will begin to lay out two different outfits the night before, thereby setting an acceptable limit on her choices.

Ages Six to Nine

With the start of school, your child will be ready to think through making decisions on his own. He will be able to grasp the concept of consequences. You can help him practice by asking him what he thinks will happen when reading a book, watching TV, or playing a game.

Ages Ten to Twelve

This age group can be dominated by impulse behavior. This is part of the awkwardness of being a preteen. Quite often, they leap before they think. You may find yourself frustrated and wondering why your preteen seems to make the correct decisions one week and not the next. You may have to slow her down and go through the steps of making a decision from time to time, just as you did when she was younger. Try to be helpful without being condescending.

Ages Thirteen to Seventeen

This age group is capable of making decisions but will often need guidance in the way the real world works. For example, your seventeen-year-old daughter claims she wants to be an artist. This is a valuable career and it's great that she has made that decision. The phrase *starving artist,* however, keeps running through your brain and the thought of her being out in the cruel world with no food to eat scares you, and rightly so. This is a time to take out your parental duct tape and keep that thought from slipping out of your mouth. Guidance, in most instances, with this age group is accepted when they ask a direct question. However, her statement about wanting to become an artist is not a direct question.

If you want her to ask direct questions, give her a real world source for information on becoming an artist. By giving outside resources to your teenager, you are letting her know that you trust her decisions and that she has choices in that field of study. You are allowing her to use all of the critical thinking skills you have taught her.

CHAPTER 5

Organizational Skills

BELIEVE IT OR NOT, the key to the most successfully organized family is the front of the refrigerator. What does yours look like? Is everyone's schedule there? Can your child look at it and know that today is his day to set the table for dinner? When you teach children to keep their schedule in a readily accessible centralized location, you're giving them permission to use their brains for other more important matters than remembering what they need to do. This time management is key in learning successful organizational skills.

Why Organization Is Important

As the main caregiver in your household, there are tasks that you complete every day, a couple of times a week, and once a month. Every day you get dressed, you make breakfast, lunch, and dinner, you change diapers, you check homework, and you straighten and clean your home. Weekly, you do laundry, grocery shop, and play chauffeur back and forth to your children's activities. Monthly, you pay bills and schedule doctor appointments. You do these tasks month after month, year after year. Mostly, you do them without thinking them through. Therein lies the problem.

Not having enough time is the largest complaint of busy families. You have to work, your children have to go to school, you all return home hungry and tired, but there is baseball practice in an hour and where is dinner? You get everyone ready, run to the nearest fast-food place, eat in the car on the way to practice, come home, check homework, and go to bed exhausted, too tired to even think about what's for dinner tomorrow. The cycle then repeats itself. You'll begin wondering, the next free minute your brain has, "Where does the time go?" or "Why can't I get anything done?"

 FACT

It is important to remember to take time out for your relationship with your spouse. Schedule dates with each other to spend time alone. Your children will benefit by learning that a loving relationship means spending time together.

This happens to every parent. You start out as individuals with your own schedules. These are easy to handle; you know what you need to do and you do them. Things change when you add other individuals to your life through marriage and family. You have things to do, your spouse has things to do, your children have things to do, and you need to mesh them all together. Then, you need to add the entire list of daily, weekly, and monthly tasks into the mix. You don't notice how hectic your life has become until you realize that you need more than twenty-four hours in a day.

Organizing Day-to-Day

Do you regularly forget to bring items you need with you? Do you often forget what day of the week it is, let alone what you need to do on that day? You're trying to remember too much. This is the key reason people become disorganized. In order to start becoming organized, you need to break yourself of this habit. Whether you are capable of remembering everything, or even some things, doesn't matter. Forcing yourself to have to remember is taking up much of your valuable time.

Start by placing the family's schedules on the refrigerator. The schedules don't have to include every single thing they plan to do, but include the major stuff and anything obvious. Use a bright colored piece of 8½-by-11-inch paper and cut it into 2-by-11-inch strips—use one strip for each person in the family. Position each strip horizontally and put each person's name on a different strip in the upper left-hand corner. Mark off seven 1½-inch blocks. At the top of each block, write the days of the week. In each block, include the most obvious things that you do, including the events that you have planned or that are recurring weekly activities. These are things that do not change often. If you work Monday, Wednesday, and Friday, write *work* on those days. If you pay your day care every Friday, write *pay day care*. If you go to a Girl Scout meeting every Monday night, write *Girl Scouts* in the Monday block. Do this for everyone in the family.

 ESSENTIAL

Fall or spring sports, holidays, and summer vacations all happen at the same time every year. So schedule them in at the beginning of every year. Does your child play fall soccer? Information on fall sports normally comes out in school fliers in the spring. So write that in on March 1. When March 1 rolls around, you'll know to be looking for the flier. You'll be able to prepare for the registration fees.

When you plot out your obvious schedule, you'll save yourself the time it takes to remember what day of the week it is. Think about it. When you get too busy, you find yourself asking, "What day of the week is it?" when you actually mean, "What do I normally do on this day?" By taking a quick glance at your obvious schedule the evening before and the morning of your day, you are sending yourself clues to be ready for that day's events. You'll avoid the time it takes to remember and gear yourself up for what's coming.

When you put up an obvious schedule for everyone in the family, there are two major benefits. They'll get the benefit of knowing what day of the week it is and you'll get the benefit of knowing what they need for their day. For example, say your school-age daughter has gym on Tuesdays and Thursdays. So the word *gym* is on her obvious schedule. When Monday night rolls around and you glance at the obvious schedule for Tuesday, you can immediately ask, "Do you have your gym bag packed?" You'll be able to prepare very calmly because it is Monday night, not Tuesday morning five minutes before the bus is supposed to arrive.

The Family Calendar

The family calendar needs to be close to your obvious schedules. When you look at one, you look at the other. All appointments, events, trips, and changes in the normal, everyday schedule need to go on the family calendar. This is a basic organizational tool. You need to take the thirty seconds it takes to write these things down. It will save you the worry and stress of thinking that you are forgetting to do something.

Encourage other family members to use the calendar also. Children as young as six years old are capable of tracking the days on the calendar and can ask you to read the events of the day. Point out the difference between the normal schedule for a day and how it changes by adding the events from the family calendar. Children who are nine years old or older can even be responsible for filling out their own events, like picture day at school or their choir concert night. Encourage this age group to also take a look at their normal daily schedule and the calendar when making plans with friends. These organizational skills will benefit the entire family.

More Organizational Tips

There are more ways to find time in your busy schedules. The good news is that you don't have to figure them all out on your own. There are experts in time management who have already done this. They have created successful time management programs and tips that you can employ in your schedule. There are books, classes, and support groups. They can be found in your community, public library, and on the Net. Employ the techniques that work best for your family.

Scheduling Household Chores

Children who have regular assigned household chores feel a sense of self-worth and competency. Household chores help give children a sense of belonging as well as teaching responsibility. They also lighten the load of housework and the feeling of "one more thing to do" that parents often feel.

When giving chores to children, allow them to pick from a list of normal household duties based on their developmental level. Post what needs to be done and when on the obvious schedule (for young children, use stickers). Remember that this is a learning process. You will need to show them what needs to be done and how to do it, probably more than once. With encouragement and time, your child will be able to take the responsibility on his own.

 QUESTION?

How much allowance should you pay your child?
This depends on how much you expect your child to pay for. One to four dollars is acceptable for a young child and up to fifteen dollars would be good for a child who is expected to pay for weekly activities with friends.

Some parents feel the obligation to pay an allowance for chores. While learning to manage money is important, paying for chores may take away the benefits of doing the chore itself. In other words, you pay an allowance to a child because learning how to manage money is an important life skill for success. They have expenses that are optional. You are allowing them to pick and choose from these expenses when you give an allowance. Outings with friends, magazine subscriptions, and extra spending money on vacation are all viable options for children to learn how to handle their money. You do chores because everyone needs to pitch in to keep the household running smoothly. If the allowance is attached to whether your child completes a chore, she may learn the wrong motivation for doing chores—for a monetary reward, rather than simply because she is part of the family.

Forming Good Habits

You are a creature of habit. What you need to be when you're a parent is a creature of "good habits." Do you wonder how some parents get so much done in a day and still have smiles on their faces? They have good habits.

A good habit is not hard to form, and breaking a bad habit isn't all that difficult either when you can replace it with a good one. There's a chemical in the brain called dopamine that controls reinforced behavior. If you stick with whatever new behavior you're trying to learn, your brain chemistry will turn it into a habit in time, normally twenty-eight to thirty days. Once something becomes a habit, it's easier to stick with it. It becomes almost second nature. You will feel uncomfortable when you don't accomplish the new behavior.

 **FACT**

A habit is something you do automatically with little, if any, forethought. It is something you do without conscious choice. Habits can be good or bad, depending on how they affect your lifestyle. Good habits will save you time, relieve tension, and increase your effectiveness. Bad habits will do just the opposite, or worse.

For example, consider this case of a healthy homework habit that one family established. One woman's children had established the habit of doing their homework immediately after school, so they could spend the rest of their evening free from that responsibility. Then one day she wasn't home when they came home from school, and the children didn't do their homework. But it bothered them so much that it was the first thing they told her when she walked in the door. So while good habits may not always result in good behavior, they do lend a hand in developing a conscience.

Juggling Career and Family

It is a day-to-day challenge when you are juggling career and family. Priorities need to be set in both areas for you to be successful in parenting your child. You need to come up with a strategy that involves serious personal choices.

Questions to Ask

Some questions you should be asking yourself about how your family will be organized include:

- Should both parents work full-time jobs?
- Should one parent work and one stay home?
- Who should work and who should stay home?
- Can you afford to live on one income?
- Should one parent work full-time and one part-time?
- Should one parent stop working while the children are young?
- Can one parent work from home? Get flextime?
- Who is getting the best medical benefits from their job?

All families face these questions and come up with their own unique answers. This is a serious personal choice. Don't allow others to impose guilt on you if you feel the need to grow as a person in your chosen profession. And don't feel that you have to answer to anyone if you choose to stay at home. When you are making your choices, consider the facts about your situation and choose what is right for you.

The Cost of Two Incomes

Many parents feel they need to work when they have small children because of economic reasons. But does it really pay if both parents work? Here is an example of the financial costs of an average American family with one small child in which the parent who would stay at home brings in $2,000 gross monthly income. You will need to plug in your own numbers, as averages differ across the nation.

Income	
Gross Monthly Income	$2,000
Expenses	
Taxes (federal, SS, state, and local)	$550
Average Child Care for an Infant/Toddler	$720
Average Cost to Commute	$125
Other Expenses (clothes, lunches, etc.)	$200
Total Second Income per Month	**$405**

If you add in the hours it takes to get ready and commute back and forth to work, because they are spent away from your child, you're talking ten-hour workdays. That's fifty hours a week, two hundred hours a month. That works out to $2.03 an hour. If you have more than one young child, you may actually be paying to go to work.

There are, of course, other reasons to work: Medical benefits and loss of professional standing are the top two reasons parents continue working. Whatever your decision is, it needs to be your decision. Remember to take all variables into consideration when making this important decision, and you'll be able to make it work for your family.

Family Time

The buzz phrase *quality family time* often brings thoughts of expectations that are too high for parents to meet. To most parents, it means concentrated, uninterrupted time to spend with their children. It is believed that this time should make up in quality for what is missed in quantity. However, most times the reality of life does not meet with those expectations, leaving parents feeling guilty and resentful—so much for "quality."

Family time is just that—any time you are spending with someone in your family. The whole family does not need to be present. If you take your daughter shopping, that's family time. If you are helping your son with his homework, that's family time. It is not just the vacations and the outings; it's every minute you spend together. Instead of trying to make the time for "quality family time," try to add quality into the "family time" you have.

Dinner is a wonderful time to spend together as a family. Considering our rushed lives, dinner is the perfect time to slow down and take a deep breath. Approval, support, and encouragement can all be found around the family dinner table. It's a great place to share your plans, talk about your day, and enjoy being with each other.

 ESSENTIAL

Whether you talk about the day's events or use it to teach manners, the family meal provides structure, continuity, and routine. During times of conflict or loss, it is a welcome certainty for the family.

Make the most of your child's sporting or school events by attending as a family and turning this into some family time. Often, siblings will want to avoid going to these events. Make it important for them to attend. This will help them learn to show support for each other; something they are going to need as they grow older and become less dependent on you.

Modeling Organizational Skills

Successful families will strive to keep their lives organized in order to be able to have time with each other. Parents can help children of all ages learn to have good organizational skills. By using communication tools such as calendars and working on good habits, you will be modeling the organizational skills your child needs for success in life.

Birth to Age Two

A newborn's life is chaotic. There is no schedule for the first few weeks. You may need to prepare older siblings for the whirlwind of life when you bring home a new baby. But as a little time goes on, schedules emerge. As your child nears the age of two, you will need to remain consistent with his schedule. For instance, naptime should be the same time every day. Vocalize his routine as you are doing it. "It's 11:30; time for lunch." This will let him know that there are certain times in the day to get things done.

Ages Three to Five

Continue to vocalize certain times of the day to this age group. They can begin to read a calendar if you use pictures or stickers on certain days. Let them check your calendar with you. Tell them the different events in the near future and allow them to cross off a day when it is finished.

Ages Six to Nine

Children in this age group benefit from having their own calendar. Colored markers and stickers make it lots of fun, too! This is also a great age to introduce a to-do list to help form good habits when they are required to do more than one task at a time. For instance, write out their morning routines in a list format, with each task on its own line. They can then check things off as they go.

Ages Ten to Twelve

Around fourth grade, schools start to provide planners for their students. Help your preteen utilize this wonderful organizational tool—she will need it. Kids in this awkward age group are often forgetful. To-do lists, planners, calendars, reminders, and big bright neon signs are all helpful. They may even need reminders to read their reminders. It's okay to keep reminding them; it will sink in eventually.

 ALERT!

> Do not try to organize your teenager's time for them. If she's spending too much time with her friends, ask her to schedule in more time for family or responsibilities. Let her choose when that time will be.

Ages Thirteen to Seventeen

Kids in this age group are capable of organizing their time. You may, however, need to help them place priorities on where to spend it. They will juggle school, family, and a social life. If you leave it entirely up to them, their social life is likely to take up 99 percent of their schedule. You will need to be firm on family time and when they need to take care of their responsibilities.

CHAPTER 6

Family Finances

WHILE YOU DO NOT NEED to have a million dollars in the bank to raise a successful child, you will need to have some financial sense. Savings and budgeting are everyday words in today's successful family.

Budgeting in Families

If the word *budget* makes you cringe, then you are not thinking of it in its correct context. Having a budget does not necessarily mean that you have to scrimp and tighten your belt; it simply is a way to keep track of your money, know where it is going, and place it where you want it to go.

When you have a family, following a budget is that much more important. Otherwise, you may feel as if your money is flying out the window faster than it is coming in. But if you stick to a budget for a month or two, you'll be able to see where your money is. This will give you an idea of where you might be able to save a few—or many—dollars that you hadn't even thought of before.

Credit/Debt Management

Many families start out in debt. Just the hospital bills for having a baby can put you there, not to mention the cost of buying a home with more bedrooms and then buying everything you need to put into them. It is imperative that you manage your credit and debt wisely. Financial problems are one of the biggest reasons parents worry. When you worry, you're frustrated. When you're frustrated, your family suffers.

Strive to be a good financial role model. Show your elder child how you are saving for big purchases. Tell him about any debts you've had and how you worked your way out of them. Open up the budget to him and allow him to give you ideas on budgeting. Financial intelligence is learned; it's not something that teenagers just pick up. In order to make sure your teenager knows how to use credit wisely, it's best to start out early and be there to help her by using good role modeling and guidelines.

 ALERT!

Reward yourself when you stay on your budget by taking advantage of the free services, classes, and fun offered in your community. Take some "me" time to give yourself a pat on the back, instead of spending the money you have just saved.

Should Your Child Have a Credit Card?

Teenagers are becoming their own market in the commerce world. It makes sense since teenagers do spend a lot of money. The credit card companies have jumped in and started offering credit cards to minors. Nearly one in seven teenagers under the age of eighteen has a credit card today. But many teenagers don't know how to manage credit and may run the risk of ending up in debt.

One main benefit of allowing your teenager to have her own credit card is the fact that you will be giving her the ability to establish a good credit rating long before she needs to apply for any loan. Therefore, you should start slowly, giving your teenager different levels of responsibility at a time. Saving and checking accounts should be started first. When your child is able to handle them responsibly, then start looking for a credit card account for her.

Considering all eighteen-year-olds can obtain a credit card without parental approval and many of these eighteen-year-olds end up in major debt because they aren't credit savvy, you should consider allowing your teenager to have a credit card early. This gives you a chance to teach her the responsibility that comes with having credit. You can choose to allow her to get a credit card solely in her name or one that is an extension of your own, if your credit company allows that.

 ESSENTIAL

You should check your credit report annually. Errors on your report could cause you a lot of trouble down the road. Make sure everything you see on the report is correct; and take the necessary steps to correct any mistakes as soon as possible.

When you expose your child to credit, you'll need to set up strict guidelines by creating an action plan. These guidelines should include when and how the credit card should be used, what types of purchases you will allow, and who is going to pay the bill. Make sure you tell your teenager about the importance of a good credit history and include that in your action plan. Keep tabs on his spending by requiring that all receipts and bills be turned over to you. Keep careful track of credit card purchases, as they can add up and hurt the family budget if they are used unwisely.

Vacation Budgets

When your family is planning a vacation, it is a good idea to set a budget for everyone's spending money. Your child can learn to budget for his own mementos and keepsakes. He can even help you budget out how much change you'll need for tolls if you're going on a long car ride. Older children and teenagers can help budget out hotel or food expenses.

Start by giving them a simple folder with blank account sheets. These will expose them to real-life ways of writing out a budget. Give them the receipts and allow them to add and subtract everything. Make sure you check their work, though, before you find out your hotel bill is higher than you thought.

Allowances

Quite a few controversies surround the ifs, whens, and whys of giving an allowance. Parents have many choices here, but first you need to understand the goal of giving an allowance. Giving your child money for him to budget and spend teaches him how to use money wisely. Allowances are not rewards for good behavior, like completing his chores, or something to be used for consequences when your child doesn't make his bed. There are other ways of disciplining those actions without taking the benefits of learning money management away. Children need this information to be successful in their money management later in life. It can only be gained through experience. When a child does not gain this experience early in life, he will make larger money management mistakes when he is on his own.

When and How to Start Giving an Allowance

In order for your child to benefit from an allowance, she needs to be able to count money, add, and subtract. This is normally learned around first and second grade. With this information, she will be capable of managing her own money but may need some guidance at first.

Before you start giving an allowance, you will need to talk about how much and what the money is for with your child. She needs to understand that the whole amount is not just for going to the store and buying candy. Part of the money should be used for one of her normal expenses, like her lunch at school. This way she'll learn about how much things cost, expenses, and how to have the money to pay for it—budgeting. For instance, if your nine-year-old daughter's school lunch costs $1.50 a day, that adds up to $7.50 a week for that expense. If you start her off with a $10 allowance and give her the responsibility of her lunch expenses, she can pay for those meals and have $2.50 to spend or save for something that she wants. You should let her know that now that she has $2.50 a week, she will be able to buy her own gum and candy at the store and that you will no longer be doing that. You need to set up the structure of giving your child an allowance and follow it religiously.

 ESSENTIAL

Give your child her allowance money on the same day of the week; give it in denominations that she can use. For instance, if she is paying for lunches, she may need it in one-dollar bills. And make sure she has a place to keep it, like a bank or a wallet.

As Your Child Gets Older

As children get older, they have more expenses that parents pay. Activities like roller-skating and the movies, magazine subscriptions, things for hobbies, and so on. Therefore, you should increase his money responsibility by increasing the amount weekly and stating what you will no longer be paying for. Be reasonable, and research how much you are actually shelling out for these things each month.

Often teenagers work a part-time job and earn quite a bit of money from it. You may begin to wonder if you should continue to pay your teen an allowance. Does he still have the expenses that his allowance was set up to pay? If so, yes, continue giving an allowance. If he is making a regular income at his job, give him some options on other expenses he can pick up. For example, his clothing or school supplies.

Be careful not to allow your teenager to have too much spending money without a purpose. Besides the fact that this can lead to all sorts of trouble behaviors, it will give your child a financial comfort zone that isn't really there. A seventeen-year-old boy who is used to being able to buy a music CD whenever he pleases because he doesn't have enough expenses attached to his money is more likely to get into financial trouble when he is nineteen years old and does have more expenses that matter. Therefore, he benefits much more if you give him his expenses and use his money to teach him financial awareness.

Saving Money

Many families, especially in these hard economic times, live paycheck to paycheck. They know that they should be saving money for this or that, but they find it hard to do so. Often, it is because they are not in the habit of saving and they think that having a savings is like having "extra," when they can't afford to have "extra." But when you have a family, saving money is not a luxury— it's a necessity.

Plan now for future expenses and develop a savings plan for each major expense. Talk to financial advisers, friends, and family about how they save. Develop ways to save money on everyday items, and then use that savings in your plan. Often, people will clip coupons for their groceries and know exactly how much they "saved" on this week's bill, but they will fail to place that "savings" into one of their savings plans.

 FACT

According to the Bureau of Labor Statistics, the tuition component of the Consumer Price Index (CPI) increased by 8 percent a year, on average, from 1979 to 2001. This means that children born today will face college costs that are three to four times current prices by the time they matriculate.

Like all good habits, saving money has to be done routinely. For instance, when the grocery clerk tells you that you saved $7.82

today, stop at the ATM on your way out and transfer $7.82 from your checking account into your savings account. Or, have someone else take it before you even see it. Many banks will put money aside in Christmas or Vacation Clubs right away if you use direct deposit. You will probably need some help looking for ideas on where you can save and how to spend wisely. *The Everything®️ Budgeting Book* has some great tips, advice, and worksheets that can help.

College Tuition

Few families can afford to pay for college for their children without some form of education financing. Parents should expect to pay at least half to two-thirds of their children's college costs through a combination of savings, current income, and loans. Therefore, it is important to start preparing as early as possible. Time is an asset when saving money. You can start the day they are born, but don't think you're too late if you haven't started yet. Today is a good day to start, even if your child is in high school.

About 529 Plans

A 529 plan is a state-run investment plan designed to help families save for future college costs. As of now, each state has at least one 529 plan.

 ALERT!

Many states waive the fee to starting a 529 plan if it is purchased in the first year of a baby's life. While the fee is nominal, generally $25, it can be a good incentive to kick-start your savings.

The main benefit to the 529 plans is the income tax breaks. All of the earnings portion of the 529 plan distributions is taxed at the student's income tax level. Therefore, as the money grows, you are not taxed on the earnings. When the money is used, it is used in your child's name and, unless your child has a high income, the taxes he pays will be much lower, because his tax rate is probably lower than yours. Congress has even given a tax-free break to all distributions until 2010.

Other benefits to the 529 plans are that the donor remains in control of the plan and other friends and family can donate to it. You decide when the money can be withdrawn and for what reasons. You can even close the account or transfer it over to another child. When family is looking for a way to give a gift for holidays or special occasions, they can send the gift directly into the account.

Scholarships and Fellowships

Scholarships and fellowships are generally given to students with special qualifications. Students who have academic, athletic, or another talent can find scholarships offered in their area of interest. These awards are also available for students who are interested in particular fields of study, minorities, and those who live in certain areas of the country or who demonstrate financial need. Local organizations also offer scholarships to those students who graduate in their area.

There are several free scholarship searches on the Internet. Do not be fooled into thinking you have to pay to get this information. Fee-based searches generally do not do any better at finding scholarships than their free alternatives. Try FastWeb at *www.fastweb.com* to start your search.

Federal Grants and Loans

A loan is a form of financial aid that must be repaid, with interest. There are several different types; however, the main ones are the Stafford and Perkins loans, PLUS (Parent Loan for Undergraduate Student) loans, and alternative or private loans. The Stafford and Perkins loan is the federal student loan. Although there is interest, it is much less than what the average interest rate would be on any other type of loan. PLUS loans are the same as student loans in that they are federally funded, only they are loans given to the parents.

FACT

Two-thirds of undergraduate students graduate with some debt, and the average federal student loan debt is $16,888. When one includes PLUS Loans in the total, the average cumulative debt incurred is $19,785.

A Federal Pell Grant, unlike a loan, does not have to be repaid. Pell Grants are awarded only to undergraduate students who have not earned a bachelor's or professional degree. For many students, Pell Grants provide a foundation of financial aid to which other aid may be added. In order to receive these federal grants or loans, you must submit the Free Application for Federal Student Aid (FAFSA). This form is available online at *www.fafsa.ed.gov*.

Insurance

When you have family, there are things that need to be insured. You need to ensure that if something should go wrong, you—or your dependents—are covered. It doesn't take too long to make sure you have the correct coverage for you and your family.

ESSENTIAL

Be sure that someone besides your spouse knows you have a life insurance plan. Name an executor to your estate and keep him or her up-to-date on your plans and where your information can be found. Ask your lawyer the best way to handle this in your area.

Life Insurance

While planning for your death may not be one of the most pleasurable things to do, it will give you peace of mind. Buying life insurance is like buying anything else. You need to shop around, compare prices and policies, and feel good about your purchase.

Here are a few tips for finding the right life insurance policy:

- Talk to people you trust. Find out what experiences your friends and family have had with different insurance carriers.
- Compare prices online with different agencies.
- Do not choose a company just because you've seen them on television or they were the first one with a great offer. The fact that a company has spent money on advertising or is able to offer you a deal doesn't mean they are best for you and your family.
- Remember that price is important, but so is security. Term life insurance can save money and provide the security you need if cost cutting is important.
- Keep your investments and your life insurance separate. There are too many scams around; keep these two things separate to avoid losing your security in a shady deal.

So, how much life insurance do you need? Well, you need to think first about the minimum amount your family would need if you or your spouse should die. What would be the monetary loss to the family's income? Take your yearly income, which is the monetary loss to the family for one year, and multiply it by however many years your children will be dependent on that income. That is the amount you should be insured for.

Auto Insurance

Auto insurance doesn't change much from when you are single to when you have a family except for two factors. The first is the fact that your family will most likely have more than one car. Generally, you can combine your insurance with your spouse's insurance.

The second factor happens when one of your children reaches driving age. You will need to inform your insurance company that there is another driver in the home. Automobile insurance policies require every licensed person in your household to be listed on your insurance policy unless he or she has a completely separate policy, including, but not limited to, teenagers and college students who use your address as their place of residence. Yes, your rates may go up. But they would be much higher if your teenager tried to insure herself.

 FACT

Auto insurance for teens costs more because of the higher risk involved, statistically speaking. According to the National Highway Safety Administration, in 1996, 6,319 young people ages fifteen to twenty died in motor vehicle crashes. Even though this age group makes up only 7 percent of the driving population, they are involved in 14 percent of all traffic fatalities.

Homeowners and Renters Insurance

Let's face it, you own a lot of stuff, and so do your children. If you do not have a decent homeowners or rental insurance policy, you could lose it all to a fire or other catastrophe with no way to replace it. The costs of replacing items damaged in a fire, earthquake, or tornado can really add up quickly, not to mention bringing more frustration to an already stressful situation. Do your research and find a policy with great coverage, and check to see if you'll need additional catastrophe insurance also. Many homeowners policies do not cover floods or earthquakes; these policies must be purchased separately if there is a danger in your area.

Being covered by a homeowners or rental insurance policy is great behavior to model for your older teenagers. You may want to show them your policy and explain rental insurance policies to them around the time they are seventeen years old. Your child will need to know about this mundane everyday living responsibility.

Retirement

When you've raised successful children, they will be successful adults when you retire. They will either be taking care of themselves or have the responsibilities of having their own families. Parents do not want to become a burden to their child at this point in their life, and rightly so. Therefore, you will need to prepare for your golden years early and make a plan for most scenarios.

Planning for retirement should begin as early as possible. This isn't often the line of thinking that parents take. They start saving for their child's college tuition and feel they will have enough time to put money away when that is done. They feel that opening an IRA, contributing to a 401(k), or belonging to a pension plan is enough. But it isn't if you don't want to be a burden to your children at this point in your life.

The first thing to do when planning your retirement is to start putting some money away. When you have enough of a nest egg, talk to a financial adviser on how to make long-term investments work for you. Get the best bang for your retirement buck by using a professional here. They will help you with what kind of taxes to expect and so much more. Next, plan out your will. If your children are still young, they do not need to be in on this discussion. As they get older though, you may want to ask their opinions; for example, what family heirlooms would they treasure, and so on. You should also look into prepaid funeral arrangements. Remember your goal is to avoid burdening your children's families, so the more you handle at a young age, the less you, and they, will have to worry about.

Check Your Resources Early and Often

It is important to check your investments at least once a month, know a roundabout figure for your Social Security, and have a handle on what you're saving in pension plans and IRAs. Your employer should be giving you yearly statements about your pension plan. If not, ask to see what you will be receiving when you retire. This figure should increase as you work longer for that company.

Check your Social Security amounts by contacting the Social Security Administration for a printout of your account. This will tell you how much you can expect to receive from Social Security when you retire. The information can be requested at ✆(800) 772-1213 or at the Social Security Administration Web site at ✒*www.ssa.gov.*

Set Goals

Retirement goals are important and fun to dream about. Parents can look forward to enjoying each other again without the responsibility of children. Although this may sound a little selfish, when you've parented your child into a successful adulthood, you deserve the time to enjoy your life. So, think about it. You may be retired for twenty to thirty years. Do you want to travel? Do you want to live someplace special? Do you want to devote some time to a personal hobby that you haven't had time for yet? You will need to keep all of these things in mind when setting your financial goals for retirement. It is easier to save money for retirement when you can envision how much you'll enjoy it.

CHAPTER 7

Emotional Intelligence

EMOTIONALLY HEALTHY CHILDREN are better at resolving conflicts, are better learners, are less likely to become involved with drugs and alcohol, have better impulse control, and have fewer behavior problems at home and at school. As you become aware of how to use your emotional intelligence as a parenting skill, your child will benefit with a healthier Emotional Quotient (EQ).

What Is Emotional Intelligence?

The world's view on intelligence has recently been given an over-haul. Some scientists and psychologists began to wonder why a person with a high IQ didn't always succeed. Why were there people with IQs over 140 sitting in jail while people with mediocre IQ levels were running multimillion-dollar corporations? Scientists and psychologists have therefore come to the conclusion that there is more than one type of intelligence. Emotional intelligence has become, as recently as the 1990s, one of these accepted types of intelligence.

Emotional intelligence, in plain English, is the ability to understand your own emotions, to understand the emotions others are feeling, and to act appropriately based on this understanding. An EQ (emotional quotient) is simply an index of how emotionally intelligent a person is, similar to an IQ, which measures intelligence.

 ESSENTIAL

Healthy emotional intelligence is clearly very important for human beings to live happy and successful lives. It helps us have empathy, set clear personal boundaries, communicate with one another, and make decisions about our lives.

Understanding Your Emotions

Understanding what emotions you're feeling isn't always as simple as it sounds. An emotion isn't just a feeling, but a more complex set of thoughts, physical states, and feelings. When you consider these three factors, you should be able to label which emotion you are experiencing. First, what are you thinking? Are your thoughts racing or are you thinking clearly? Do you know what is causing this emotion? Second, what is your body doing physically? Is your heart racing? Is your breath even? Third, what base feelings do you feel? Are they strong? Are they pleasant or unpleasant? Taking all of this into account, you should be able to identify your emotion.

How you label the emotion you are feeling will give you clues as to how to act. Think of it this way: How often have you felt you were getting angry when in fact you were becoming frustrated? Anger is a tough emotion to manage. When you label the emotion you are feeling as anger, you've given yourself a roadblock that can lead to more frustration, which will lead to true anger. If you can recognize that you are frustrated, you'll set yourself up to look for a solution because you likely know better how to handle frustration. Parents deal with frustration on a daily basis. This is why labeling what we are truly feeling is so important to our emotional health.

Here is a list of pleasant and unpleasant emotions you can use for labeling. Think about each one and the differences between the meanings of each one.

Unpleasant Emotions	Pleasant Emotions
Agitated	Confident
Confused	Excited
Dejected	Fascinated
Disappointed	Grateful
Frazzled	Gratified
Frustrated	Happy
Melancholic	Hopeful
Stressed	Optimistic
Uneasy	Secure
Worried	Thrilled

Understanding Emotions Others Are Feeling

In order to truly understand what emotional state another person is in, you would need to be inside their head. There are clues, however, and emotionally intelligent people are capable of picking up on those clues. By doing so, they can label the emotion the other person is feeling and gauge their responses to that person appropriately.

Body language and tone of voice tend to be the clearest clues to another's emotional state. For instance, if your small child walks into the room in midafternoon asking when dinner will be ready while rubbing his eyes and yawning, you know he is hungry and tired, and therefore, grumpy. You're able to respond quickly by offering him a snack and some quiet time with a video. It really doesn't take a rocket scientist to begin to recognize how others are feeling. It's human nature to do this. But it does take some trial and error to alter our responses accordingly.

Acting Appropriately Based on Understanding Emotions

Acting appropriately while feeling strong emotional urges can be the hardest part of healthy emotional intelligence. As all parents can testify, you will feel every emotion there is to feel while parenting your child. There will be times when your feelings need to be put aside while problems are dealt with and solutions are found. This is why emotional intelligence is such an important parenting skill.

If, for example, your son scores the winning touchdown in his last football game of the season, you'll feel ecstatic! You'll be cheering louder than anyone else in the stands. But the second you see him, you'll have to remember that he does not want you to kiss his whole face in front of all of his friends—that would be embarrassing. You'll have to wait to show him how proud you are of him. Perhaps a big hug and a celebration dinner later would be better.

Learning appropriate responses to your children's achievements and disappointments will be a lifelong process; it's not an exact science. The uniqueness of each individual plays a role. For instance if your son is more sensitive and cries more often than your daughter, you may not be as worried when you come upon him crying as you would if you found your daughter in tears. Therefore, your reaction will be different.

What Is Your EQ?

Try this simple emotional intelligence test to measure your EQ.

For each statement, answer *very true, mostly true, somewhat true, mostly not true,* or *not true.*

1. Once I finish a good cry, I feel much better.
2. Often I get sad or depressed.
3. I am comfortable hugging friends and family of either sex.
4. I have angry feelings when dealing with certain people.
5. I do my very best even when there is no one else to see it or praise it.
6. People who are angry or emotional make me feel uncomfortable.
7. I am comfortable saying "I love you" to men, women, and children whom I love.
8. I sometimes become jealous.
9. I have a need to make a difference not only for my family but also for strangers.
10. I feel as though people's reactions often come clear out of the blue.

To score the test, separate the odd questions from the even ones. For the odd questions, give yourself 5 points for *very true,* 4 points for *mostly true,* 3 points for *somewhat true,* 2 points for *mostly not true,* and 1 point for *not true.* For the even questions, give yourself 5 points for *not true,* 4 points for *mostly not true,* 3 points for *somewhat true,* 2 points for *mostly true,* and 1 point for *very true.*

A score of more than 35 shows that you have a basic understanding of your emotions and you are comfortable working with them. A lower score does not mean that you have no emotions or emotional sense. It does mean that you should take some time to get in touch with your feelings more often. You may want to try examining different situations and your emotional reactions to those situations. Simply take ten minutes at the end of your day and go over what feelings you had and what caused them.

 **FACT**

There is no standard test for measuring EQ as there is for measuring IQ. Many simple tests measure how well you know your own feelings or how well you can read the feelings of others, but they do not measure how you would act in those situations.

Become Aware of Your Child's EQ

Through every stage of childhood development, your child is working on her emotional intelligence. Even the frustrated two-year-old who is throwing a temper tantrum is learning to manage her emotions. Keep in mind that the road to development has bumps. Also, it is always wise to remember that developing healthy emotional intelligence is an ongoing process; it is not set in stone at birth but is learned through experiences with yourself and others.

By becoming aware of your child's emotional intelligence, while allowing for the bumps of child development, you will be more in tune with how she is doing in terms of learning the skills emotional intelligence teaches. Some of these skills are empathy, communication with others, cooperation, and resolution of conflicts. These are separate and distinct skills, but they all require an emotionally intelligent person to master them.

Empathy is the ability to understand someone else's feelings and take his or her perspective without being overcome by your own emotions. This clearly ties into communicating with others. An emotionally intelligent person is able to express his or her concerns or problems without being drawn into the other person's feelings, thus making it easier to cooperate and resolve conflicts. Clear communication will help the emotionally intelligent person know when to take the lead and when to follow or when it is a good time to stand firm or give in.

 ESSENTIAL

Children have basic emotional needs that need to be met on a daily basis in order for their emotional intelligence to thrive. Some of these needs are to be accepted, to feel accomplishment, to feel cared about and loved, to be reassured and understood, and to feel supported and trusted.

In the next few years, you are going to be hearing more and more about emotional intelligence. Be on the lookout for parenting classes and books on how to help your children build their emotional intelligence.

Strengthening Your EQ

When you strengthen your emotional intelligence, you become more self-aware, you are better able to manage and resolve conflicts, you communicate better, and you have more empathy. All of these achievements are key skills to success. You can strengthen them by paying close attention to what you are feeling and how you react to those feelings on a daily basis.

Take time out nightly to think about your day; you could even keep notes in a journal. Think about what feelings you had and what set them off. What were your reactions to those feelings? Would you change your reaction now that you've had time to contemplate it? Were you self-aware? Don't use this time to beat yourself up over any mistakes you may have made during your day. Know that you did your best and are looking to do even better. Congratulate yourself on the times you were self-aware and your actions showed it.

Next think about how your child was feeling that day. Can you name his feelings? What were his reactions to those feelings? What were your reactions? Were you able not to become overwhelmed by his feelings? Allowing your child to own his feelings and label them correctly will help him manage his reactions.

 ALERT!

Try not to analyze everything your child says and does while working on building his emotional intelligence. Build slowly or your child may get frustrated at your overanalyzing and start rejecting your attempts.

Stress and Emotional Intelligence

Because using emotional intelligence is the opposite of making rash decisions, you can also strengthen your emotional intelligence by reducing stress. Everyone has to deal with the everyday ups and downs of life. The trick is to keep stress where it belongs—outside your emotions.

When you internalize stress, you compound it. Emotionally intelligent people realize that change is natural and don't mind normal day-to-day stress as an outside influence on them. They do not internalize stress. Therefore, they find solutions without being overcome by emotions.

Your children will benefit from your not internalizing everyday stress by being able to enjoy a parent who doesn't have knee-jerk reactions to changes. For example, if the scout meeting runs late, he still wants to be asked how it went, rather than hear a list of things you should be doing instead of waiting around for him. Don't get hung up on the fact that your schedule has not gone exactly according to your plan. Be flexible, accept the change (in this case, the unexpected lateness), and move on.

Talk to Yourself

Believe it or not, it's healthy to talk to yourself. Verbalizing what you are feeling will help your intellectual side understand your emotional side. It will help you catch when you are not sending yourself positive messages. It will help you see clearly the solutions to the problems you are facing. Even if you know how to tackle a problem, verbalizing it will give you confidence that you are going in the right direction.

Reaching Your Limits

Children are not perfect as adults are not perfect. They sometimes get frustrated and yell, stomp their feet, boss around their siblings, and so on. This does not make them hotheaded, immature, or bossy. There is a difference between telling your child she is *acting* immaturely and telling her she *is* immature. In the latter, you are using a label. Labels are detrimental to your child's emotional intelligence. Parents tend to use labels when they have reached their limit of frustration. When you're feeling frustrated, catch yourself and take a deep breath before speaking.

 ESSENTIAL

Positive thinking goes a long way toward controlling emotions. Minute meditations and affirmations can help bring you out of an unpleasant emotion. Start with "I can" or "I am able to" and end with the action you want to accomplish.

Children reach their limits of frustration also. There will be times when your normally passive and empathetic son will rip a toy out of his younger sister's hands with no regard for the elephant tears that are rolling down her face. There are many reasons for such actions; fatigue and stress are just a couple. These are triggers. You'll need to take care of them first. Then, you can discuss how he made his sister feel by taking the toy away from her when things have calmed down, even if it is the next day.

Try not to be too dramatic. Yelling and making a scene when your child is not acting appropriately is not using your emotional intelligence. Find the triggers for the overwhelming feelings that cause these reactions and take a preventive approach next time.

Your child's emotional intelligence is not black or white. He will go through shades of gray and may almost be perfect one day and a tyrant the next. Learn to go with his flow and keep an eye out for triggers.

Modeling a Healthy EQ

When your child observes you taking a deep breath, verbalizing what emotion you are feeling and what you can do about the task at hand, she will slowly learn that she can also label her emotions correctly and find solutions to her problems without becoming overwhelmed. It will become a habit that will benefit her throughout her entire life. She will continually be able to build on the foundation you have given her and become an emotionally intelligent person.

 FACT

In modeling a healthy EQ, you actually need to model your emotions, not just your actions. Children are in tune with how their parents are feeling, so faking an emotion will not fool them. It will only teach them to fake it.

Birth to Age Two

By the age of six months, babies are capable of distinguishing among different facial expressions and imitating them. Verbalize your emotions when you smile or frown. Begin to teach your child empathy by telling him you are sorry that he is sad when he is crying.

One- to two-year-olds have the ability to show affection. They have strong feelings for their parents and will show anxiety when separated from them. They will begin to show pride in their accomplishments and show displeasure at the loss of an object such as a toy.

Ages Three to Five

Children in this stage become more aware of themselves as individuals and they begin to compare themselves with others. They also start to verbalize the feelings other people are having in their favorite books or television shows. As they near the end of this age range, they will be able to express what other people are feeling. This will help them with new friendships.

One of the main goals for children in this stage is to learn how to share and cooperate. This goes hand in hand with their newly acquired ability to show moral reasoning, because they are able to understand why it is wrong to take something from someone. They know what hurt feelings feel like and know that it is not nice to hurt someone's feelings.

Ages Six to Nine

Children in this age group are interested in rules and rituals; they have a strong desire to do what is right. They view the world in black and white. Therefore, they have a hard time finding empathy when someone does something wrong. They also have a hard time with failure and have a genuine need for approval. Many times you can change your child's melancholy mood to a happier one just by praising her.

You'll find that your child has a best friend and an enemy at these ages. As she is now capable of seeing things from another's point of view, you may want to question her choices in friends or enemies gently to get a perspective on what she finds important in other people. Don't be too critical though. Children in this age range are still fairly self-centered.

Ages Ten to Twelve

Around the age of ten, children stop thinking in black and white and begin to start seeing everything in rainbows of every shade of color. When this happens, your child will begin to have opinions, and he will share them—with you and everyone else. At this age, children become emotionally involved with their opinions. An emotionally intelligent parent, or any parent who wants to keep hold of their sanity, will respect the fact that their child has a right to his opinion and will teach him how to agree to disagree. They will gently remind their child that other people have a right to their perspectives, too. They will guide their child toward respect for others even when their opinions aren't the same. While this stage may cause quite a bit of frustration, take some time out and enjoy what is really going on. Your child is learning how to think for himself. This is as monumental a task as when he took his first steps. It can also be as treacherous! So use your emotional intelligence to make a clear path for him.

 ESSENTIAL

The most important thing you can do for your teenager is always communicate with her. While talking about tough issues isn't always comfortable, it is always needed. You'll find that when you feel comfortable talking to your teen, she will become more comfortable talking to you.

Ages Thirteen to Seventeen

Older children can distinguish between the small differences in emotions. They have had enough experiences to know the difference between sad and miserable, happy and thrilled, or confused and frazzled. They understand their own feelings and are able to analyze them. Ask them their opinion often.

Teenagers begin to have close relationships with other people. They form strong friendships and have the ability to fall in love. As your teenage gets older, it is appropriate to start discussing the differences between like, lust, and love. The more she understands the difference between these emotions, the better prepared she will be when faced with them.

CHAPTER 8

Self-Control and Self-Discipline

N O DOUBT ABOUT IT, life's little frustrations grow exponentially when you're a parent. While you can't always control your emotions, you can control your behaviors. Working on your self-control and learning some self-discipline techniques will help you handle even the most stressful times.

Why They Matter

Demonstrating self-control and self-discipline is quite challenging for both parents and children. You need to learn to put your desires and emotions aside in order to choose appropriate actions that will benefit both you and your child. This is not an easy task since your desires and emotions are what tend to drive your behaviors.

Take, for example, the first week you brought your baby home from the hospital. You desired sleep, but your baby desired to be fed in the middle of the night. Since a week-old baby is not able to control his hunger, your desires did not coincide. So, you chose to get out of bed and feed your baby. You did so without throwing a fit about being awakened. You accepted your baby's needs; therefore, you put your desires and emotions aside and took appropriate actions. You showed good self-control and self-discipline.

As with all of the key parenting skills, learning and demonstrating self-control and self-discipline is important for both the parent and the child. It is a skill you will both use many times every day. As you use your self-control and self-discipline skills, you will find that they become a habit, leading to more positive outcomes and a successful relationship between you and your child.

Self-Control Deals with Emotions

Self-control is the ability to make choices about how to behave and act rather than relying on impulses that are based on your emotions or desires. It is not the absence of your emotions or desires. They are often still present. Self-control means thinking about the consequences of an action before taking that action, and then choosing the most appropriate action to take, even when your emotions might be pushing you to take a different action.

 ESSENTIAL

To help you choose appropriate actions, start by identifying the emotions you are feeling. Strong emotions parents report feeling when dealing with their children include love, anger, frustration, happiness, pride, fear, jealousy, grief, and sadness.

Although using self-control may appear to be easy, when you add strong emotions pushing you toward impulse behavior, it isn't easy at all. The strong emotional bond parents feel with their children is unsurpassed and can sometimes be overwhelming. It can be difficult to say no to a child who is begging for something you've denied him at a time when you are already feeling stressed—it would be so easy to just give in. If you can manage good self-control, however, you'll be able to turn down the child's request without losing your temper.

Self-Discipline Deals with Personal Improvement

Right from the start you have learned to make knowledgeable choices, to become independent, to follow rules, to believe in yourself, to enjoy learning, and to have good values and beliefs. In other words, you have been learning self-discipline. But have you been practicing what you've learned or have you just been caught up in the everyday grind?

You told your child to adhere to the rules, but do you wear your seat belt in the car even on short trips? You've told your child that reading is fun, but when was the last time you picked up a book "just for fun"? You've told your child to respect others, but do you complain about your boss or coworkers at the dinner table? How about your mother-in-law? "Do as I say, not as I do" doesn't work. It never has and it never will!

As a parent, you have the ability to see your own flaws as you are bringing up your child. Don't ignore them! Recognizing your faults presents you with an opportunity to work on your own self-control and self-discipline. It will enrich your life. All parents have areas in which they can better themselves.

Self-Control and Self-Discipline Work Together

It takes making good choices based on thinking through the consequences (self-control) to learn valuable lessons that enrich our lives (self-discipline). Self-discipline depends on self-control. Of course, self-control was a lot easier when you only had to worry about yourself.

There are no tried–and-true measurements of the ramifications to your self-control when you become a parent. Some parents handle strong emotions better than others. They are capable of remaining calm in most instances. But all parents, whether they admit it or not, have some room to strengthen their self-control and self-discipline.

Life's Little Frustrations

Life can be really stressful. There are so many decisions to make. There is so much to get done. Changes in routine can feel like a heavy weight on your shoulders—worse if you don't have a routine. There is a lot of pressure from many different angles when you are a parent. Often you don't realize that you're getting excessively frustrated until you lose your self-control.

There are ways to prevent these little frustrations from leading to a loss of self-control. Many are just part of a healthy lifestyle. Others take some thought and practice. Although these suggestions will not eliminate all stress from your life, they will make you capable of handling the little frustrations that pile up to create huge stressors.

Live a Healthy Lifestyle

Get your rest. Your body isn't capable of handling any type of stress well when it is tired. Go to bed at a decent hour so you can wake up refreshed in the morning.

Eat well. This doesn't mean you have to turn into a health-food junkie, although a balanced diet is important. It means to eat regular meals at regular times. It means to slow down and enjoy those meals. Don't skip breakfast. Don't work through lunch. Sit down and enjoy dinner with the entire family.

 ALERT!

Caffeine, smoking, alcohol, and high sugar intake should be avoided. While they seem to help relieve stress, or people tend to turn to them when they are feeling stressed, they will only add to your stress levels.

Exercise. Regular physical activities provide a natural way to release tension in the body and will often lead to an automatic state of relaxation. Exercising is a great way to relieve stress.

Learn to Say No

Are you a people pleaser? Do you say yes when you wanted to say no? Are you the parent the PTA president comes running to every time she needs someone to head a committee? Do you end up resenting things you volunteered to do because you feel pushed into doing them? Then you need to learn to say no and drop the guilt. Although volunteering to help other people is commendable, overloading your schedule will increase your stress levels.

Six simple ways to say no:

1. "No" while shaking your head.
2. "No, I won't be able to help with that."
3. "No, I already have a commitment for that time."
4. "No, I'm not taking on any more volunteer work at this time."
5. "No, I'm not able to provide the required commitment level."
6. "No. I'm unable to schedule things that far ahead."

If you noticed, each one of the answers started with the word *no*. Get it out of your mouth first so you are committed to the answer. Say your answer in a friendly tone but firmly. If you feel yourself being drawn into a discussion over the matter, repeat your answer, still being friendly, but more firmly.

 ESSENTIAL

If you feel the need to soften your "no," you can add "I'm sorry." Just do not feel that you owe anyone a long explanation. You don't have to debate your reasons with anyone.

Always Have a Plan B

By recognizing that stress is an inevitable part of life, you prepare yourself to cope with it. Therefore, you can learn to be flexible in your personal and professional life by always having a backup plan. For example, at home, always have a meal that can go from freezer to oven in case you forget to take dinner out of the freezer ahead of time. At work, talk with your boss about how you plan to handle snow days, days when your child is sick, if the nurse calls from school, and other emergencies before they happen. Your boss will appreciate your advance planning, and you can relax because the decisions are already made about how to handle these things if and when they come up.

Pick Your Battles

When you pick your battles, you are putting things in perspective. Often things are not as important as they seem at first. You need to prioritize what you would like to see from your child and give it that level of attention. If you give all behaviors you expect from your child the same level of priority, you will only cause needless stress for both of you.

Try this activity. Take ten minutes every evening and write down each time your child caused you stress. Write down the behavior and your reaction. Prioritize your child's behaviors in terms of importance—for example, safety issues are the most important, clean hands are the least important. Then write down if your reaction matched the priority. There is no need to share this information with anyone else, so you can be honest with yourself. Next, write down what you could have done differently in the situations that caused you stress. In the morning, reread what you wrote. Learn from it before you start your new day. In a week's time, you will find yourself prioritizing your child's behavior before you react.

Lashing Out

It is important for you to remain in control of yourself when you are dealing with a situation with your child and you've become angry. Losing control and lashing out will only escalate any situation. Yelling is often a sign that you have run out of other more productive ways of handling a problem. Hitting is simply unacceptable. Whatever side of the spanking debate you are on, you know that hitting your child out of anger is not the right thing to do.

 **FACT**

According to the American Academy of Pediatrics, parents are more likely to use aversive techniques of discipline when they are angry or stressed. In 44 percent of those surveyed, corporal punishment was used *more than* 50 percent of the time because the parent lost his or her temper. As many as 85 percent of those surveyed expressed moderate to high anger while punishing their children. These findings challenge most the notion that parents can spank in a calm manner.

When you do lose your temper, restore good feelings and reconnect with your child as soon as you feel calm and capable. Apologizing will not diminish your authority. It will teach your child that everyone makes mistakes. It will show your child that you respect them and the importance of saying "I'm sorry."

Ten Alternatives to Lashing Out

When you begin to feel stressed and pressured to the point where you may lash out at your child—Stop! Try one of these options instead:

- Take a step back and remember that you are the adult.
- Close your eyes and imagine you're hearing what your child is about to hear.
- Close your eyes and count backward from twenty.
- Take out a photo album and concentrate on happier times.
- If another adult is there, walk away and let him or her take over.
- Take a hot bath or splash cold water on your face.
- Go for a walk and handle the situation when you get back.

- Turn on some music and sing along.
- Pick up a pencil and write down as many helpful words as you can think of or journal about what got you to this frustrating point.
- Phone a friend.

Activities That Calm

Although you have learned how to prevent stress, there are times when you will become frustrated. It's not good to carry this frustration around. It will take up too much of your energy, cause you to be tense, and possibly lead to problems with your relationships. Don't worry! There are plenty of ways to relieve stress.

 ESSENTIAL

Although many people associate the term *stress* with psychological stress, physicians use this term to denote any force that impairs the stability and balance of bodily functions. By definition, exercise is stressful, but its health benefits are unquestionable. Some stress is good, as long as it doesn't overwhelm you.

Laugh More

Research has shown that laughter has an effective and specific role in the reduction of tension resulting from stress. It is nearly impossible to feel tense while laughing. The better the laugh, the lower the tension and the more long-lasting the relief. Long after the laughter has ended, body tensions continue to decrease. Laughter is better than a quick fix. Your stress level may stay at its reduced state for as long as an hour after a good laugh.

The ability to laugh will give you the ability to recognize and appreciate the humor of life's idiosyncrasies. A good laugh provides a cleansing of emotions and release of emotional tension. So keep a good book with humorous stories around or read the daily comics and get your daily dose of stress-reducing laughter.

 **FACT**

Prior to age six, children seem to enjoy their own inventions of humor. The humor tends to be spontaneous and original. At age six, children begin to show an interest in ready-made jokes. This interest continues to develop between the ages of seven and ten. This age group delights in trying to stump adults with knock-knock jokes and riddles.

Tell Someone

Find support in someone you trust. Whether it's a friend, a parent facing similar problems, or a support group, you may relieve some tension by getting your problems "off your chest." Oftentimes, just saying a problem out loud will help you deal with it.

Of course, do not unload your frustrations to a friend in front of your child, particularly if he is part of the problem. This will cause your child to feel shame, which will lower his self-esteem.

Deep Breathing

This technique works wonderfully for immediate stress relief. Before reacting to something that is stressing you, breathe deeply and slowly for three breaths. To get the right rhythm, count to ten in your head as you are breathing in and again as you are breathing out. If you have time, sit comfortably, close your eyes, and breathe slowly and deeply for two full minutes. Concentrate fully on the breathing.

Play

Getting lost in a good game of hide-and-seek with your child, or enjoying your favorite hobby without your child, may be just what you need to distract you from your frustrations. It will allow your mind to take a break and just enjoy the moment. Then when you need to go back to the problem at hand, you will be able to tackle it more calmly.

Affirmations

Affirmations are simple statements you say to yourself that help to insert positive ideas and suggestions into your subconscious. This is a form of constructive self-talk that can be very effective, if done properly. The key to the effectiveness of this method of stress reduction is the frequent repetition of these positive statements while keeping your mind clear of negative thoughts. Say the affirmations softly to yourself so that your subconscious can take in these thoughts and begin to act on them automatically.

You will find this positive thinking technique to be surprisingly helpful. By focusing on positive changes you want to make in your behavior, you will be capable of bringing about that positive behavior. By saying the affirmations out loud to yourself, you are reaffirming the behavior you wish to change or improve.

You can easily create your own affirmations. Simply start with, "I am capable . . ." and fill in the behavior you would like to achieve. Here are some examples:

- "I am capable of being calm."
- "I am capable of being happy."
- "I am capable of being a successful parent."

Modeling Self-Control and Self-Discipline

By modeling self-control and self-discipline, you are giving your child examples to emulate. You will give yourself a sense of competency in your own life. You will be able to help yourself keep your overemotional responses in check. You will be able to focus your efforts on letting go of the things you cannot change in your life so that you can concentrate on the things you can change. All the while, you will be teaching these wonderful things to your child by example.

As with all aspects of growing up, the lessons of self-control and self-discipline should be age-appropriate. However, the following guidelines are just that—guidelines. Remember to take into account your child's individualism.

Birth to Age Two

Infants and toddlers are often frustrated because there's a large discrepancy between the things they *want* to do and what they are *capable* of doing while remaining safe. Children this age can often be distracted from frustrating situations with fun activities or toys. By the end of this age, children understand the word *no* and will most likely be using it quite frequently. Short time-outs are appropriate for two-year-olds.

Ages Three to Five

Children in this age group are seeking more independence, but they won't allow you to go too far. Time-outs are appropriate. A rule of thumb for the amount of time to have your child sit is one minute for every year in age up to five minutes. Encourage your child to take deep breaths when she needs to calm down.

Ages Six to Nine

At this age your child is beginning to understand that he can control his behavior and make choices. Encourage your child to stop and think about the choices he has when faced with a problem. You may offer some alternative options, but allow him to make the choice. Deep breathing and play are wonderful relaxation techniques for this age group. Time-outs still work, but they could be moved to allowing the child to sit in his own private space.

Ages Ten to Twelve

Children in this age group are starting to think less in terms of black and white, and more in shades of gray. You will find yourself wondering just how many shades there could possibly be. You are going to find yourself in some wild debates over the different choices they have and why they lead to certain consequences. This is good for your child's critical thinking skills and can be encouraged within reason. Just make sure the consequences for her actions remain clear.

This age is often associated with moodiness, especially for girls who are entering puberty. Again, some leeway needs to be given within reason. Suggest quiet activities such as listening to music or journaling for relaxation.

Ages Thirteen to Seventeen

This age group is capable of self-control. They understand consequences, although they are not very good at evaluating the long-term consequences of their actions. They know what the long-term consequences are, even though those consequences may hold little weight in the choice a teenager will make. Therefore, you may want to set up short-term consequences for behaviors you deem important. Encourage your child to talk through problem situations. Teach him the value of your chosen relaxation techniques.

CHAPTER 9

Morals and Values

WHAT PARENTS DON'T WANT to teach their children the fundamental morals and values of honesty, integrity, kindness, and responsibility (among other things)? These morals and values are needed on the road to being successful. When parents examine their own personal morals and values, and learn how to coach their children, they turn these into a valuable parenting skill.

The Difference Between Morals and Values

Values are principles that are considered worthwhile and desirable in someone's character, like honesty or respectfulness. Morals are concerned with the judgment of principles of right and wrong, or with values, in relation to human action and character. For example, honesty is a value. Therefore, it is morally wrong to lie. The two work hand in hand, but they are not the same.

When you hear about children having moral fiber, it means they have a core set of values and are able to use them to make morally correct decisions in their day-to-day lives. They make these decisions because it is the right thing to do, not because they will benefit in any particular way. Many times making the correct decision based on morals is taking the harder road; the easy way is often the quickest way out of an unfortunate situation.

ALERT!

Your child's moral fiber is based on the core set of values she has been taught from birth. Children who are not taught basic fundamental values have a harder time with relationships and do not take responsibility for their actions.

Unfortunately, sometimes even when people have strong morals, their actions can come across to their children as a double standard. Parents ask their children to do one thing, but they do something else. For example, you expect your children to be honest, but you called your boss and told him you would not be coming into work because you are sick, when truthfully you just wanted to spend the day with a friend. You feel that this is okay because your boss has an unfair policy on taking time off. Therefore, you're teaching your children that it is okay to lie to people who are being unfair to you. The next week your teenager takes a day off from school saying he is sick. You find out that he really took the day because there was a test he was unprepared for. When you ask him what happened, he tells you that he felt the teacher was being unfair in giving such a hard test for one reason or another. Would you connect the two instances?

ESSENTIAL

Set reasonable expectations when teaching your children morals and values. Note what they are capable of developmentally. A small child may be able to voice that an action is bad, but she may not totally understand *why* that action is bad.

Many times when your child is doing something morally wrong, especially when you know he has the fundamental value needed to do what is right, he is modeling behavior he has seen in his home. He is acting on his observations of moral decisions made by the adults around him. Again, the morally correct thing to do is often the harder road to take. Children need to see their parents take the harder road because it is the right thing to do. They need to observe the benefits of strengthening their moral fiber. They need you to show them.

Why Successful Children Need Both

Children who grow up with consistent and positive values are happier and do better with relationships. They are also more likely to contribute something valuable to society. These are all signs of a successful person.

 FACT

Trust your child to do the right thing within the limits of your child's age and stage of development. If you continually expect him to do the wrong thing, he will comply by doing exactly what you're expecting. Children want to please; allow them to do so.

Children who understand their values are able to make moral decisions based on them. For instance, if your eight-year-old child understands that taking responsibility for her actions is important, she is likely to speak up when she accidentally breaks something at school. Because she showed this integrity, her teacher will be able to trust her when she says she wasn't responsible for the next mishap. This strengthens her relationship with her teacher, which promotes good learning experiences in her classroom.

Establishing Your Values

Generally, you are going to want your child to have the values you find important, the ones that have worked for you throughout your life. Have you ever taken a good look at what they are? Identifying the values you find important is the first step in teaching your values to your children. Take some time to list values that are most important to you. Brainstorm as many as you can think of and write them down as they come to you. The order doesn't matter. Then after you've run out of ideas, go back and prioritize the list from most to least important. Here are a few to start with:

- *Cleanliness*—A habit of keeping clean.
- *Compassion*—Deep awareness of the suffering of another coupled with the wish to relieve it.
- *Courage*—The state of mind that enables one to face danger or fear with confidence.
- *Friendliness*—A state of being likeable to another person, enjoyment in their company.
- *Honesty*—The quality or state of being truthful.
- *Integrity*—Moral soundness; honesty; freedom from corrupting influence.
- *Kindness*—The quality of being warm-hearted, considerate, humane, and sympathetic.
- *Perseverance*—Steady persistence in adhering to a course of action or a purpose.
- *Promptness*—Being on time, punctual.
- *Responsibility*—The state, quality, or fact of being accountable.

When you have a handle on which values you find most important for yourself, go back and make another list of the values you want your child to have. List the reasons you want your child to have each value, and how you feel he will benefit. Once you have clearly defined what you want your child to learn from you, it will be easier to find a course of action in your day-to-day life.

Religious Values

Many parents obtain support from their churches, synagogues, mosques, or other religious institutions. This promotes a sense of belonging. Children, and adults, learn and strengthen their morals and values because of the confidence their church group provides. Not only can your church teach lessons about your religion; it is also a great place to meet other adults and children who share your values. Get your child involved in the youth areas of your church, and they will have friends and peers with the same values as their family.

 **QUESTION?**

Will religious involvement really help your child?
A belief in God or a higher being enables a child to feel responsibility for her actions. She gains a sense of security that there is someone watching over her and helping to guide her. From that security, she gains confidence that her actions have meaning.

Family Values

Family values are what tie a family together. They complete a sense of belonging to a family. If you set clear family values for your children, they will have a guide to know how they are expected to act to belong to their family.

If you are having trouble trying to think about what your family values are, try finishing this statement, "Our family believes in . . . A few examples:

- Sticking up for one another.
- Spending time together.
- Going to church.
- Being patriotic.

If your child has a hard time telling you what his family values are, that is a clear sign you are not verbalizing them enough. Look for opportunities to say them out loud. Rephrase normal everyday activities and add the value in. For example say, "Let's go to the store and spend some time together" instead of "Let's go to the store."

 ESSENTIAL

Make it a habit to go over your family values weekly with your children. Clear communication of family values will enable your children to live by them and be proud of them.

Teaching Values Through Stories

Aesop's fables and other virtue stories highlight values. In order for the value to be taught, however, you will need to help. Your child will come to the moral conclusion. But if she is given the chance to think a story through, so that she can come up with the moral on her own, she'll remember it better and will have processed it enough to use it in her daily life. It may also give you some insights into what's going on in your child's mind.

Aesop's "The Tortoise and the Hare" is a good example. The story goes like this: A tortoise challenges a hare to a race. The hare laughs and boasts because he knows he is faster than the tortoise and he will win. The hare goes really fast, but then he decides he can take a nice nap and still beat the tortoise. So he falls asleep along the way. The tortoise passes him and wins the race while the hare is still sleeping. So, what is the moral of the story? What value does it teach?

Actually, there is more than one answer. If you give your child the opportunity to tell you what she thinks the lesson is, you'll see what she thought was important in the story. If you simply just tell her the story is about not being boastful, you may miss the fact that she thinks it's about working hard to get to the finish line.

Enter into Your Child's World of Play

As children begin dramatic play, using the world of pretend, you have an opportunity to teach values. Enter into this world with them by allowing them to guide you. Ask questions about the rules in their place of make-believe. Are there good guys and bad guys? What makes the good guys good? What makes the bad guys bad? Why is their baby crying? You can have fun and teach your child valuable lessons at the same time.

Teachable Moments

There are teachable moments all the time, every day. If your child comes home from school and regales you with a story about how Billy threw his apple at Suzy at lunch recess, you have found a teachable moment. The trick is not to lecture but to help your child come around to the correct conclusion by asking questions. If you can get your child to verbalize that throwing an apple at someone is not right because it hurts, he will have learned a lesson. If you lecture him about how bad Billy is for doing that to Suzy, the lesson he will have learned is not to tell you what happens at school.

Teachable moments have value over stories from books because children are the participants in the production of the moment. They can associate themselves with the players and see themselves facing the same or similar dilemmas. Ask your child how she would have handled the situation if she were in it. Let her role-play both sides of the dilemma.

Dinnertime is another teachable moment in your family's day. Children learn how to share and ask for advice around the dinner table. They learn how to speak to each other with respect. As a family, they learn to resolve conflicts. There are many lessons to be learned while the family sits and breaks bread together.

When Your Values Differ from Your Partner's

Values and the importance placed on them differ from person to person. Some people place a higher moral emphasis on honesty than promptness. But a boss who constantly has to wait for an employee who is late may not care whether that employee is honest with his excuse—he just wants him there on time.

Your values may differ greatly from your partner's. If you think about the one thing that really annoys you about your partner, you will be able to identify a value difference the two of you have. This is okay! You can still come to an agreement on what value you want to teach your child.

For instance, say one of you is very neat and clean, while the other tends to save everything and clutter abounds in your home. You can still teach your child to be neat and organized by giving him examples from the partner who is neat and organized. The secret is to talk to your partner and decide what you want to teach your child. Then, without guilt, teach it together. You don't have to be perfect to teach your child to be better than you.

Pluralism and Tolerance

In America's multicultural society, it is important to remain aware of your attitudes toward people of different cultures and backgrounds. There will be times when your children may be faced with value questions because of the differences in some values in cultures other than your own. For example, Muslim girls may wear head coverings in their high school. Your child will need to learn acceptance of this practice without voicing an opinion toward those who practice it. Tolerance of all cultures is beneficial to everyone as a whole.

Problems arise when parents state their opinions of other cultures without thinking or, even worse, thinking and not caring. Children will pick up on these opinions and form attitudes that will not help them grow. Your children's world will be even more diverse than yours. Allow your child to learn acceptance and pluralism to help him succeed in society.

Modeling Your Morals and Values

Like everything with children, morals and values will develop over time, as children develop the role they play in the world around them. An infant who is practicing her grasping reflex on her sibling's hair is not going to understand that she should not pull hair because pulling hair hurts. A five-year-old, on the other hand, can be made to understand that pulling hair is the wrong way to get his sibling's attention.

Birth to Age Two

Children in this stage are living in the "me" world. They are learning what they like and dislike as it is happening to them. They may not be able to put the term *friendly* to a smile from your grocery store clerk, but they know they like it when someone smiles at them. Toward the middle of this stage, they will be returning this smile and modeling friendly behavior. As they reach the age of two, they are capable of learning the language that teaches values and morals. Praise them with phrases that verbalize the value and how they demonstrated the value. For example, "It was very kind of you to share your toy." Although children in this age group will not know yet what being kind means to the other person, they will know that "kind" is how they are acting.

Ages Three to Five

Children in this stage are developing a sense of "the other." They know that the people around them are separate from them and that the actions they take have an effect on other people. They begin to realize that being kind makes other people happy. Along the same lines, they know that being mean makes other people sad or angry. Their actions may stem from how they want another person to feel. If you think about the phrase, "Misery loves company," you will understand this.

Children in this age group do not yet realize that their actions will come back to haunt them. Therefore, they need verbal reminders from you. Point out when they are being unkind as well as when they are being kind. Show them the benefits of being kind, honest, or fair by verbalizing how others are responding to them.

 **FACT**

According to the American Academy of Child and Adolescent Psychology, it is normal for a very young child to take something that excites his or her interest. This should not be regarded as stealing until the child is old enough, usually at three to five years, to understand that taking something that belongs to another person is wrong.

Ages Six to Nine

Kids in this age group begin to gain a firm grasp of how their actions affect other people and how it in turn affects them. They will start to do things to see others' reactions to them. Coupled with the sense of knowing right from wrong, children this age really want to please. They thrive on praise. Now is a good time to introduce values with more difficult concepts. *Perseverance, good sportsmanship,* and *fair play* are a little harder to understand than *being truthful.* Therefore, point out examples of these values in everyday life. This is easier to do as your child starts his formal education and likes talking about what is happening during his day.

Television shows often provide opportunities to talk about values with your six- to nine-year-old. Asking questions about how someone feels and why they did what they did will provide you with insights to how your child perceives the world around him. He will be able to tell you who did what wrong, but he may not be able to see why someone did a particular thing and he will most likely not care. He sees things in black and white and cannot understand the concept of doing something wrong for the "right reasons."

Ages Ten to Twelve

This age group is capable of seeing the subtleties of right and wrong. They are able to debate each side of a moral question. They enjoy taking a look at everyday issues and trying on an opinion. They often switch sides of an issue depending on the information they are receiving. They will often become inflexible in their opinion if you challenge it directly without offering new information that could change it. Try to show them all sides of an issue without giving your own opinion. Allow them to ask questions about each part, exploring the issue fully. Just because they are asking questions doesn't necessarily mean that they agree with any particular opinion. They simply have a strong need to know.

It is very important that parents allow self-expression among kids in this age group. Do your best not to shut their thinking down by giving your opinion too readily or strongly. Your child is learning how to be an individual in this stage and will learn to respect other people's opinions when they see this modeled by their parents respecting their opinions.

Ages Thirteen to Seventeen

Teenagers are constantly questioning and revamping their value systems. The media showers them with how wonderful it is to be sexy, drugs are rampant in high school hallways, and doing well in school is often ridiculed. Is it any wonder parents feel the stress of the uphill battle of teaching decent values? Along the same lines, your teenager is also feeling this stress.

This age group not only can see things from all sides and form an opinion but after some time that opinion becomes part of their identity. Parents who allow their children to have parties where alcohol is available promote the opinion that it's okay to drink when you're sixteen years old. Their reasoning is that "everybody does it." This behavior shows teenagers the easy road to having fun instead of encouraging enjoyment without the influence of a mood-altering drug. When you have to take a stand on an unpleasant topic, be sure to communicate clearly and firmly why you have made that decision and the values behind it.

CHAPTER 10

Creating Useful Parenting Tools

I T IS OFTEN SAID that parenting is the hardest job in the world, and it comes without a manual. While this is certainly true, there is certainly no shortage of advice out there on every aspect of parenting. But how do you know whose advice to trust? Parents who understand the uniqueness of their family and seek out the right advice are capable of using it to create useful parenting tools that will lead to their child's success.

Listening to the Experts

There are numerous reasons some people are considered parenting experts. Perhaps they've raised ten children. Or maybe they have chosen child psychology as their field of study. Whatever the reason, there is good advice to be found from these experts. The trick is to follow the advice that feels right to you and disengage from the advice that doesn't seem to fit.

Often parents wonder where to look or whom to ask. The answer is everywhere and everyone. Just because you ask for advice doesn't mean you must follow it. But if you don't ask or continue looking, you may miss a solution to your problem.

Information in Print

Start at your local library or a bookstore that allows you to sit down and browse through a book without having to buy it first. Read a chapter or two and get a feel for the author. Who is he? Has he been where you are? Does the book offer simple solutions or complex theory? Both have their advantages. Compare and contrast different styles of books before you commit to reading them in their entirety. When you find a book you feel will be helpful, buy it, so that you always have it on hand when you need it.

Once you get the book home, read it through once highlighting areas that you want to look at again. Make notes in the margins of the book about why you think or do not think the advice will work for your family. Be picky about which advice you choose to use with your family. Just because the author hits the nail on the head for you with one recommendation doesn't mean you should turn the whole book into your family bible. Your children are unique and you will need to find what fits for them in each specific area.

 ESSENTIAL

Parenting advice books are not family heirlooms. When you invest the money for one, use it to the fullest extend by highlighting sections, writing your thoughts in it, and keeping it within easy access for when you need it again.

So, how do you know when something fits? Often, you don't know until you try it out. Read the advice through more than once to be sure you understand what the author is suggesting, and then test it out with your child. Test it out fully and give the suggestion time to take root and work.

Tidbits of advice can also be found in parenting magazines or psychological journals. Again, your library has these and it is easier on the family budget. You will also get into the habit of actually reading the material if you go to the library first. Often people subscribe to these types of magazines with every good intention of using them only to find them stacking up unread. But, if you find that you are enjoying the same magazine time and time again, by all means, buy a subscription.

The Internet is also a powerful source of information for parents. While the media tends to hype the negative side of surfing the Net, do not let that stop you from using it. After all, a place where you can go and read through the American Academy of Child and Adolescent Psychology *Facts for Families Series* (✎*www.aacap.org*) can't be all that bad.

 QUESTION?

Where can you find parenting sites on the Internet?
Two recommended Internet sites for parents are the family hub at About.com where there are specific parenting sites for different ages and needs, and Disney's Family.com, where different experts contribute to a wide range of parenting topics.

Your Child's Pediatrician

It is imperative to have an open and honest relationship with your child's pediatrician. While you may learn more about teething or the common cold than you ever expected to know, you will never become a medical expert. Even medical experts often do not choose to treat their own children. When it comes to medical concerns, you have to rely on your child's doctor, so choose wisely. Here are a few questions you can ask them to help you decide if they are a good fit for your child:

- What is your pediatric background?
- What hospitals are you associated with?
- If I have a minor question, is it okay to call?
- Up to what age do you see children?
- How quickly are you able to see a sick child?

- If my child gets sick in the middle of the night, do you have on-call services?
- What is the scheduled length of your appointments?
- Do you use any physician assistants? If I feel the need, will I be able to request to see you instead?
- What is your position on breastfeeding/using antibiotics/other important topics?
- How much are your fees for office visits? What types of insurance do you accept?

 **FACT**

According to the AAP, pediatricians are doctors who "focus on the physical, emotional, and social health of infants, children, adolescents, and young adults from birth to twenty-one years. Their patient-care lens is focused on prevention, detection, and management of physical, behavioral, developmental, and social problems that affect children."

Do not be afraid to ask questions of your child's pediatrician when you don't understand something or feel you would like an alternate choice in treatment. If the medical diagnosis for your child is serious, a second opinion is advisable. Ask your child's pediatrician for names of doctors who specialize in that area.

Specialists

Parents often view doctors who are specialists as people who know everything. The truth of the matter is they know a lot about one particular area—their specialty. When they give you suggestions that fall into their area of expertise, follow them. When they go off on a tangent and give you general advice, you may want to check with your child's pediatrician before following it.

Doctors who specialize do not have a lot of time, so come prepared with your questions. Write the answers down so that you can look them over later; you may be anxious and not able to remember important facts.

Listening to Family, Friends, and Neighbors

A strong extended family support system can give you confidence when it comes to parenting your children. Although it may seem like everyone from Great-Uncle Walter to your own mother are telling you what to do, in truth, they are just trying to be helpful. Ultimately, you have the choice whether to follow their suggestions. If you do, make sure it is for the right reasons. Don't feel guilty because the person who gave the advice may be hurt or upset if you don't follow it. Again, trust your instincts. You are the expert on *your* family.

 ESSENTIAL

You do not have to report back to the family how a problem is going or whether you took their advice. If they ask and you prefer not to talk about it, be general in your answer and thank them again for their advice.

When friends and neighbors get into the mix, things can go haywire. Always be open to what they have to say and give each piece of advice some thought, but don't be pressured into following the advice. Teenagers are not the only beings who can be pressured by peers. When you joined the ranks of parents around the world, you got a new set of peers who have ideas and suggestions on everything from what schools your child should attend to making the perfect cinnamon toast. Pick and choose what is right for you.

Don't Give Away Your Child's Secrets

Often when there is a problem you are seeking advice for, it involves personal information about your child. Sometimes parents become so emotionally distraught over a problem they are facing with their child that they gab about it to everyone who will listen. Even though you do this with the good intention of getting some advice, this can be an invasion of your child's privacy. As a parent, you'll need to respect that. If you are at a loss for solutions, ask someone privately. Ask her to keep it to herself. You're the one your child asked for this advice. Never talk about your child's problem out loud in front of her. This will cause shame.

 **FACT**

As your child gets older, he will begin to feel the need for more privacy, especially from you. Allow him privacy, but communicate clearly that if you feel he is being unsafe, it is not only your right, but it is your responsibility as a parent to find out what is going on through whatever means necessary.

How to Use Good Advice

When you receive good advice, whether it comes from books or family and friends, introduce it to your family slowly. If you make sudden changes, you run the risk of your children rejecting it without giving it a chance. Here's an example: You walk in the door one night and announce to your family that you have just read this great article on how too much television reduces a child's IQ and how reading increases it. Consequently, you have decided to throw away the television and get everyone library cards instead. This approach will probably not bring about the desired result of getting your child to read more. Sometimes, you need to take an indirect route.

On the other hand, if the issue with your child concerns safety, the direct approach works very well. Say, for example, your teenager has been caught driving recklessly. You will need to seek out advice on this problem and communicate what you expect of her clearly, directly, and as soon as possible.

The Indirect Route of Using Advice

Nowhere in the parenting rules does it state that you have to tell your child everything. You own the reasons for your decisions, and you do not have to share them. Take, for example, a child who will not go within ten feet of a vegetable but loves lasagna. If you make the decision to put a light layer of spinach into your next lasagna, you do not need to ever share that decision. If your child notices, by all means confess. But chances are that a child who will not eat vegetables has a problem with the thought of them rather than the taste of them.

This is not to say that you should trick your child. Using advice indirectly just means that you don't have to lay out every decision like a play-by-play game plan. Remember that you are making decisions for your family's benefit. So if something goes awry and doesn't work, don't feel guilty. Just move on and try something else.

ALERT!

Never lie to your children. If there is something you feel they do not need to know, then tell them that. Lying to your children will cause them to lose trust in you.

The Direct Route of Using Advice

Sharing with your family that you have received some advice that you feel will work in handling a problem your family is facing and then showing them the game plan is the direct use of sharing advice. Allow everyone in the family to have some input on how the advice is implemented, but remain determined to give the suggestion a try. Do not forget to share the benefits of solving the problem by using that particular game plan.

Information Overload

Sometimes too much of a good thing is just simply too much. If you are an information junkie and do everything by the book, you will miss out on the wonder of your children. Try not to overanalyze and try to trust your own instincts first, before you go and look for answers elsewhere.

Information overload is a type of stress generated by an overwhelming amount of input, which must be processed or acted on. It can happen to parents easily when they are dealing with finding answers to problems their children are experiencing.

Information overload can cause undue stress. It can cause you to be unhappy with situations that are really perfectly fine. In the 1950s it was thought that left-handed children should be taught how to write with their right hand. The experts believed that left-handedness was a defect. Parents watched their children become overwhelmingly stressed-out over trying to perform neat handwriting with their nondominant hand. Although this change made most parents uncomfortable, they trusted the information they received and forced the issue with their children. We now know that left-handedness is not a defect and that many parents suspected this all along.

You are your child's expert. Trust your instincts and be picky about what advice you take to heart. Always be willing to try out new suggestions, but change back if they aren't working or if they bring about other problems.

Becoming Your Own Expert

When you want to do a better job at work, you learn more about your job and apply that learning to your daily tasks. Parenting should be looked at in much the same way. But there are no prerequisites to becoming a parent. Often people believe they have the ability to parent just because they had the physical ability to have a child. Therefore, they are not open to learning the skills and tools it takes to raise a successful child.

As a successful parent, however, you know that there are no boundaries to how much you can learn about parenting. There is always something more that you can do to make life easier or better for your child. You know that becoming your own expert on your family means you need to learn continually and to adjust what you've learned about parenting. You also know that you are capable of it.

Support Groups

It is wise to seek out other parents who have the same values and goals for their children as you do. You can then turn to them for support for everyday frustrations or if life should throw you a curveball. Parenting support groups come in all flavors. There are some groups based on particular parenting philosophies, or you could choose a general group at your church or community center. The benefits of a general group are twofold. First, you are more apt to find someone with your parenting style. Second, these kinds of groups often run classes or have speakers at their meetings. Therefore, you will have more opportunities to learn.

You can also become a part of a parenting support group without leaving the comfort of your home. Parenting sites on the Internet often have community bulletin boards where you can ask questions, give your opinion, and get more information. Many people have found this type of support best because their identity remains semiprivate and they won't run into the people they told their problems to at the grocery store.

 ALERT!

Be careful with your private information when you sign up to post on a parenting support bulletin board. Read the company's privacy statement and use a free e-mail service instead of the one from your ISP. This will cut down on junk e-mail at your main e-mail address.

Keep Your Information Organized

It never fails that the minute you want to reread something, you can't find it. For instance, if you've saved an article on questions to ask your son's teacher at the school's parents' night, you'll need to make sure you have it handy when parents' night comes around. For articles and magazines, keep a three-ring binder with five sleeves. Mark them: Education Tips, Communication Tips, Discipline Tips, Fun Activities, and Miscellaneous. Put this binder on a shelf with your other parenting books. Fill it as you go by cutting or printing out articles. Once every week pull it out and reread something that interests you.

Five Key Parenting Tools

There are five key parenting tools that will help you lead your child to success. If you study them and continue to strive toward making them work for your family, your child will learn the attributes he needs to succeed in life. Each key parenting tool leaves room for different family structures and cultural differences. Each tool has the ability to be tweaked to fit your uniqueness. Many of these tools wouldn't work without the touch of your parenting style. Each of these tools is covered in more detail in the chapters that follow.

Modeling

Modeling is the basis of learning through observation. By learning more about modeling, you will be able to use this tool to teach your child how you expect him to behave. By definition, this means you will have to take a look at your own behavior. Modeling is part of the reason our children truly do make us better people.

Communication

There are many different types of communication tools available to parents, but the most important thing to remember is to communicate! Communicate daily—both verbally and nonverbally. Hugs and smiles are communication and children need lots of them.

Discipline

Discipline isn't about punishment. It's the way you handle what is expected of your children and the choices they make. While discipline isn't something parents enjoy, it is a necessary part of parenting.

Problem-Solving

Successful parents become very good at problem-solving. They even become capable of solving more than one problem at a time. This ability is very useful because more often than not you will have to solve multiple problems simultaneously, especially if you have more than one child.

Family Traditions

Family traditions are a parenting tool that we often take for granted. They show your child that she belongs in her family. She is a part of it. Having a sense of belonging will teach your child good character and the ability to love. Learn to use your family's traditions as an effective parenting tool.

CHAPTER 11

Modeling

C HILDREN ARE BORN COPYCATS! Imitating is one of the first methods children employ to learn about their world. The experts term this learning technique *modeling*. Perhaps the most important thing you can do for your child, from the time she is born, is to model the behavior you want to see in her.

Learning Through Behavior Modeling

Behavior modeling is observational learning. Children learn by observing the people in the world around them. When your infant observes you smiling, he will learn to smile. When your toddler watches you throw a ball, she will learn to throw a ball. When your three-year-old observes you using colorful language with a telemarketer on the phone, he will enjoy repeating that phrase on his next phone call with Grandma.

Yes! Children are always observing and, therefore, always learning. They are tuned not only into what you are doing but also into your emotions. If you get angry and start slamming pots and pans because you burned dinner, your son will learn not only that slamming pots and pans is an acceptable behavior when you're angry, but also that burning dinner is reason enough to be angry. This is all the more reason to learn as much as you can about behavior modeling. A successful parent will use this observational learning process to her advantage. She will turn it into a useful parenting tool.

 ESSENTIAL

> Don't think you'll ever fool them. Your children know you better than anyone in this world. If you are sad, tell them you're sad, and if you can, why. If you choose to tell them that nothing is wrong, you will be teaching them the unhealthy practice of burying their feelings.

The History Behind Modeling

Modeling comes from cognitive psychologist Albert Bandura's social learning theory, or social cognitive theory. He believed that people acquire behaviors through the observation of others and then imitate what they have observed. One of his most famous studies involved the Bobo doll, an inflatable, egg-shaped doll that was weighted on the bottom so you could punch it and it would wobble but not fall over. It always returned to its upright position. At the time of the study, Bobo the clown was painted on the doll. The study group consisted of a woman, Bobo, and a group of kindergartners. The woman punched Bobo saying "Sockeroo," hit him with a hammer, sat on him, and kicked him. The children giggled and enjoyed watching her play with the toy. They were then led to an observational playroom that had a brand-new Bobo in it. The children proceeded to beat the daylights out of poor Bobo, obviously imitating the woman, even saying "Sockeroo" when punching him.

This, and hundreds of other studies like it, led Bandura to develop his theory. In his book, *Self-Efficacy: The Exercise of Control*, he explains how so much of the learning that people do is based on observation of others' behavior. People don't have to rely solely on the effects of their own actions to learn how to behave. Observing others helps people see how new behaviors are performed, so that even if they don't imitate that behavior immediately, they have it filed away in their minds for the time when they do confront a new situation where the behavior can be applied. Observational learning can be broken into four underlying component processes.

Will Modeling Work?

The first two underlying processes that make modeling work are observational. They are attention and retention. In order for a child to learn anything, he needs to be paying attention to the behavior. If he is sleepy or grumpy, he will not be paying attention and will not grasp the full scope of what is happening. Therefore, he will not be able to imitate it. Likewise, if the child is not able to remember the behavior—retention—he will also not be able to imitate it.

The second two underlying processes are reactional. They are reproduction and motivation. In order to model a behavior, the child must be capable of reproducing it. A boy who watches his father hit a home run in baseball may be able to swing a bat but not yet have the eye-hand coordination it takes to hit the ball. Fortunately, a person's ability to reproduce a behavior improves with practice. If the father praises his son on his efforts, he will be providing motivation to continue that particular behavior. Through this practice-praise cycle, the son will someday learn to hit the ball and possibly imitate his father's home run.

 **FACT**

The social learning theory has been used to help psychologists and other researchers understand aggression and psychological disorders, particularly issues in behavior modification. It is also the theoretical foundation for the technique of behavior modeling that is widely used in many training programs.

The Role of Role Models

A role model is someone your child wants to emulate. It could be a teacher, a famous athlete, a pop star, or your next-door neighbor. Role models come in all shapes and sizes. They do all kinds of jobs. The only thing they have in common is that to the child who is looking up to them, they inspire awe.

Children begin to mimic role models at an early age. You can easily see this when you introduce a four-year-old to a story about a superhero. The thought of being able to fly around the world and save humanity from the evildoers is awe-inspiring. Now, if the super-hero wears a cape and shouts, "Up, up, and away" when he takes off into flight, it will not be long before the four-year-old is tying a sheet around his neck and springing up off his bed shouting in a similar manner. But most important, this child will want to save the world. He'll feel confident that he has the ability because his role model does. Even if the goal is unrealistic, the confidence his role model inspired is not.

As children grow older, their role models become more real-istic. They'll begin searching for successful people in their areas of interest. The one thing that will not change as their search for a role model matures is the confidence they gain through having a role model. While the latest pop star may seem like a valid role model to a youth, you may want to sway her in other directions. There are interesting people in every field of study and walk of life. It is worth the time and effort to find a fitting role model to teach your child about.

Parental Influence

You are your child's first role model. You provide every need for your young child, including being that first role model. As your child grows, she will want to dress like you, talk like you, and act like you. She will even begin to use your intonation and body lan-guage when quoting one of your phrases. This will normally make you feel proud and make for wonderful stories to share with friends and family.

As all good things must come to an end, however, your child will grow out of wanting to be you because she will begin to have other influences in her life. She will start to try on other identities, use phrases and words that her peer group has coined and—horror of horrors—she may even roll her eyes at you. You will wonder what happened to the child who believed you were the end-all and be-all of her world. Don't fret! Believe it or not, your influence is still there.

Recent studies have shown that while peer influence peaks during middle adolescence, parents still maintain an edge where it matters most—in morals and values. A survey on birth control use conducted by the Princeton Survey Research Associates for the Henry J. Kaiser Family Foundation found that parents rate high among many teens as trustworthy and preferred information sources on birth control. One in two teens said they "trust" their parents most for reliable and complete information about birth control; only 12 percent said they trust a friend the most.

Often your influence is indirect; teenagers tend to seek out friends who are from similar social and cultural backgrounds with the same fundamental values and beliefs. Therefore, peers actually tend to reinforce parental values. From this perspective, peer influence is positive and motivating.

Peer Influence

Peers are friends or acquaintances who are around the same age. Your child interacts with his peers at school, at church, at basketball practice, everywhere he goes. Peers influence your child's life just by spending time with him. Your child will learn by modeling things they do, just as they will learn by modeling what your child does. This is human nature. We all listen to and learn from other people in our own age group.

As your child grows older, peers will become increasingly important. You will start to see signs of this growing peer influence when your preteen daughter starts to want clothes the same style as her friends have or begins to be obsessed with the newest teen idol because everyone else at school is. This is normal. The need to fit in and feel like part of the group peaks during early adolescence. So much so that a preteen's self-esteem is directly affected by the degree to which she feels part of her peer group.

 ESSENTIAL

Role-play can be an important preventive tool for parents who want to teach their teenagers how to combat negative peer pressure. Show your teen how to say no by giving her the actions and words.

Parents tend to think of peer influence in the negative sense. They worry about their children being influenced by peers and that they may try some things that they normally wouldn't try on their own. This is a well-founded worry and something you will need to keep an eye on. However, remember that much of the peer influence surrounding your child is positive and healthy. For example, a teenage boy who wants to impress the teenage girls in his peer group will begin to improve his hygiene. His parents will go from chasing him into the shower once a week to wondering how high their water bill is going to be.

The upswing of peer influence in the preteen years is a sign of children beginning to break away from their parents and forming their own identity. You can help maintain a positive peer influence for them by:

- Keeping them in activities that they enjoy, such as sports, youth groups, school clubs, and so on.
- Encouraging them to make decisions as much as possible.

- Praising them when they make wise choices.
- Being sensitive and tolerant, and never too far away from your sense of humor.

 FACT

You cannot pick your child's friends, but you can pick the pools of people from which they pick their friends. Get them involved in youth organizations in your community or church, organized sports, and scouting groups. If you want to peek into your child's individuality, get involved with him.

Do as I Say, Not as I Do

Think about your worst habit. Your child will probably pick it up. If you are prone to gossiping, your child will most likely be prone to gossiping. You may see this behavior in your child and let her know that gossiping isn't a behavior that you want to see from her. If she is older, she may point out to you your own behavior with that infamous line: "But you do it." The worst part about this statement is you know that she is right. The only way to fix that is to change your own behavior.

In order for a child to be successful, you need to become successful as a parent. You need to drop your bad habits and strive to become a better person. You need to continue to grow and never stop reaching for your own goals. You don't need to be perfect, but you do need to consistently strive to be better.

Drop the Guilt

There will be times when your child will model a behavior of yours that you dislike. Or he will pick up a habit of yours that you wish you didn't have. There is absolutely no sense in beating yourself up over it. Feeling guilty will only lead to poor decisions about modifying the behavior and a lower sense of self-esteem for both you and your child.

If you want to change the behavior in your child, you will have to make an effort to change the behavior in yourself. The best way to do this is together! First, admit to your child that you need to change this bad habit and you are hoping that he will decide to also. Then, come up with a plan together to replace the bad habit with a good habit. Use praise and rewards when the good habit is demonstrated. Remember that it will take some time for the bad habit to go away totally, so don't worry about little slip-ups.

Mentors

A mentor is defined as a wise and trusted counselor or teacher. Generally, a mentor is someone your child can look up to and learn a specific skill from. While role models can often be mentors, usually a mentor is someone who takes a more active role in your child's life. For instance, Hank Aaron is a wonderful role model for your son if he is interested in baseball. But, his baseball coach or an older boy on his team will most likely play the role of his mentor.

 ALERT!

It is important for you to have open communication with your child's mentor. While we like to think that all coaches, teachers, and youth leaders are wonderful people, unfortunately, some are not. Introduce yourself as soon as possible so that you will feel comfortable talking to him or her if you have any concerns.

Statistics show that mentoring helps a child improve school attendance and performance and boosts the child's likelihood of attending college. And, children with mentors are less likely to use drugs or alcohol. While some associate mentors with children who are disadvantaged, virtually all children, and adults, can benefit from having a mentor.

Some famous mentor pairs are:

- Marion Ross—mentor to Henry Winkler
- Jonathan Winters—mentor to Robin Williams
- Madonna—mentor to Gwyneth Paltrow
- Whitney Houston—mentor to Brandi
- Aristotle—mentor to Alexander the Great
- Dr. Martin Luther King Jr.—mentor to Jesse Jackson

When you begin to look for a mentor, think first about what specific things you are looking for. If your child has an interest in becoming a doctor, find someone in that field of study who can help her. If your child needs someone to talk to or just spend some time with, then look for a responsible adult who is willing to play that role—extended family are a wonderful resource for this role! Or there are community organizations that offer mentor programs for kids of all ages, such as the Big Brothers/Big Sisters program. If you are looking for a mentoring program for your child, start with the National Mentoring Center: ☎(800) 547-6339, ext. 135.

 **FACT**

An independent study conducted by Public Private Ventures in 1995 found that children who were paired with mentors were 46 percent less likely to begin using illegal drugs, 27 percent less likely to begin using alcohol, and 52 percent less likely to skip school.

The Natural Progression of Modeling

When you use modeling as a parenting tool, your children will start to copy you in ways you may not immediately see. This tool will help, or hinder, their advancement according to their development. Remember to monitor your own behavior and keep your sense of humor.

Birth to Age Two

Infants take in everything and will begin to imitate what you do. As they grow, you can practice simple movements with them such as blowing kisses, clapping their hands, and waving. Their ability to imitate your actions will increase as their motor skills grow.

Ages Three to Five

Preschool children are capable of modeling expressions along with behaviors. They may start imitating feelings that you express, even though they may not truly feel the same way. They will also start using another's "tone of voice" from time to time. They may be imitating you or they may begin to imitate others in their lives, such as siblings, a day-care worker, or a grandparent.

Children this age begin to develop friendships. They start to join their peers in playing games, express more awareness of other children's feelings, share toys, and compare themselves with others.

 ESSENTIAL

Show your preschooler how to act, so she has something to imitate. Children this age learn best by being shown exactly what to do. If you give them the words and actions, they will learn the concept. For example, handing someone something and saying, "I'll share this with you" teaches cooperation.

Ages Six to Nine

Children this age have a longer attention span and tend to be very interested in rules and rituals. They tend to be able to retain more of what they observe and can imitate complex habits that you or others perform. If an older sibling comes home from school, sharpens her pencil, and begins her homework right away, your six- to nine-year-old will want to do the same. This is a wonderful time to develop or tweak everyday routines.

Being with friends becomes increasingly important. Your child will seek security in groups, will enjoy organized play, and will benefit from being in an organized club at this age. Although he will still be somewhat self-centered, he can see another person's point of view. He will also begin to distinguish between people he likes and people he doesn't like. He may have a best friend and an enemy.

Ages Ten to Twelve

Preteens start to look outside the family to "try on" different behaviors to see if they are comfortable with them. They will flip-flop between these different behaviors; they may like something one day and hate it the next. They are starting their search for their identity.

Ages Thirteen to Seventeen

Role models and mentors are extremely important in this stage. Although teenagers are still modeling different behaviors and trying on new identities, you will start to see some of these behaviors stick. This is because your teenager has found value in these behaviors. Therefore, she feels they fit and makes them a part of who she is. The more you surround your teen with people whose behavior you feel is worth emulating, the happier you'll be with the behavior choices she makes.

CHAPTER 12

Communication Tools

ALL THE EXPERTS AGREE—clear communication is an optimum tool when parenting. There are times, however, when the phrase *clear communication* may seem like an oxymoron. Don't fret! Using a few tips and tricks, you will be able to place this tool in your parenting toolbox.

Children Need Open Communication

Learning to communicate effectively with your child could be the single most important thing you do for them. Effective communication opens doors between you and your child. It will bring you closer together and strengthen your relationship. When your child feels he can come to you with a problem, or just give you an account of his day, he will feel secure that you care enough to listen to him. This will give him confidence and help boost his self-esteem.

Ongoing Communication

Communication with your child does not have a start time and an end time—it is all of the time. Your body language when you make her breakfast communicates something to her. Your mannerism when you answer the phone communicates to her. You do not have to

be in a direct conversation with her to be communicating what you think and feel.

To communicate your love for your child, remember that actions speak louder than words. Express your affection with smiles and hugs. Say good morning daily and spend time tucking your child in nightly. Support her interests by being there when she plays in a game or is involved in another function. Write love notes and leave them on her bed, in her lunch box, or anyplace else you know she'll find them.

 FACT

It is also important to maintain ongoing communication with the people in your child's life. Research shows that children do better in school when parents talk often with teachers and do not just rely on conferences to find out what is going on at school.

Body Language

Even an infant uses body language. Stance, facial expressions, and other nonverbal signs are capable of being understood by children and adults. Your body language says what you do not say verbally. It will also give you away if you lie about your feelings. Your child will be able to pick up on this faster than anyone; he uses your body language as a clue to gauge you right from the beginning.

Always communicate honestly about how you are feeling, even if what you are feeling isn't pleasant. If you verbalize the unpleasant feeling and then explain how you are going to try to fix it, you will teach your child that it is okay to have unpleasant feelings and that people are capable of controlling their feelings. For instance, you could say, "Mommy is frustrated right now, but I'm going to take a minute to calm down."

Without Judgment

When you judge your child, you rip at her self-esteem and at your relationship. While your opinion is important, you need to know that your opinion can have the same effect as a bull in a china shop. Use nonjudgmental words when expressing how you feel. Show respect by accepting your child's right to her feelings. Remember to criticize your child's actions rather than your child. Reassure her that you know she is capable even when she has made a mistake.

Dream the Dreams of Childhood

The hopes and dreams of childhood fade in time into the aspirations of adulthood. While this is a natural process and one that propels you toward the goals you have set for yourself in life, there is something to be missed when this happens. Parents are lucky enough to be able to experience these hopes and dreams for a second time.

When your child is sharing his hopes and dreams with you, there is no room for practicality. Life doesn't always have to be figured out on the spot. Enjoy his imaginings and share some of your own.

National Communicate with Your Kids Day

A little-known observance is National Communicate with Your Kids Day, which is celebrated on December 5. Although you should strive to communicate better with your child every day, you may want to set aside some time on this day to talk with your family about how you all can communicate better. Find out what suggestions your children have and write them down. Set a goal and make a date to check how you are doing on your goal. Even the youngest in the family can work on a goal such as saying something nice to someone every day.

Door Openers versus Door Slammers

One important listening skill to have when communicating with your child is being certain to use "door openers," as opposed to "door slammers." Door openers are open-ended responses that do not convey evaluation or judgment. Door slammers are just the opposite; they convey to your child that you do not wish to have this discussion with her. They make her feel guilty for wanting to know. They shut the door on any communication.

Some examples of door openers include:

- "What do you think?"
- "Would you like to share more about that?"
- "That's a good question."
- "I don't know, but I'll find out."
- "I'm interested in what you are saying."
- "Do you know what that means?"
- "That sounds important to you."
- "Do you want to talk about it?"
- "I'm here when you want to talk."

Some examples of door slammers include:

- "Don't talk to me in that tone of voice!"
- "No."
- "You are too young to understand."
- "If you say that again, I'll . . . "
- "That's none of your business."
- "I don't care what your friends are doing!"
- "We'll talk about that when you need to know."
- "That's just for boys/girls."
- "Why are you asking me that?"
- "You don't need to know about that."

Active Listening

An important skill for parents to master is active listening. When parents listen actively, they send children the message that they are important enough to have the parent's undivided attention. Many problems can be solved and even prevented when parents take the time to use active listening. Importantly, when a parent is an active listener, she is able to guide children to solve problems for themselves.

In order to listen actively, you need to face your child, look him in the eye, and give him your undivided attention. Give him time to express his entire concern without making any comments. Repeat back to him what you think you heard him say. Ask him open-ended questions and use door-opener statements to get a better understanding of what he wants. When you can repeat back to him what you think he wants and he agrees, give him choices about what can happen and ask what choice he thinks would be best.

 ESSENTIAL

Actions speak louder than words. If you want your child to listen in a calm manner, you have to act in a calm manner. Trying to communicate when you have too many other things on your mind will only send the wrong signals to your child.

When using active listening, it is important not to let emotions get in the way. If your child is expressing frustration when she comes to you, do not put her off until she has calmed down. She may just need you to listen to her to diffuse her frustration. On the other hand, you cannot permit her to be disrespectful to you. In a case such as this, you can convey that you are here for her just as soon as she is ready to talk to you respectfully.

Lecturing

You can remember the days of old where there was only one thing worse than getting grounded—the lecture! At some time, your parents decided to become modern parents and learned that talking to their children about what was wrong was more effective than punishment. Now, millions of people brought up in the 1970s and 1980s dread the lecture, for good reason. It tends to be a one-sided conversation that doesn't actually accomplish anything.

There are times, however, when a form of "the lecture" is an appropriate communication tool. The time for this format of conversation is when your child "needs to know" something, usually some new understanding about the way society works or on a serious topic such as sex. It is a time when there is information about life or the world that they need the facts on. It is open communication in that your child is able to ask questions, but it is part lecture in that you not only need to impart information but should add your opinion as well. Your opinion, when given respectfully, is important to your children. Studies show they do value what you think, especially about your family values.

 **FACT**

Sometimes all your child wants is your attention. He will interrupt you or misbehave to get it if he has to. Create a routine where you set aside some time during the day to listen actively to him, so that he doesn't have to resort to misbehavior to get what he wants. Do this routine every day.

A need-to-know lecture will probably start out just like any other conversation that you have with your child. She will ask a question and you will respond by having her clarify what it is she actually wants. The difference comes when you realize the magnitude of what she is asking. When you have open communication with your child, she will ask life-altering questions. It is your job as her parent to give her the information she needs to make informed decisions. This is the lecture part of your conversation. The rest of it remains open communication.

Once you've decided a need-to-know lecture is appropriate, set aside some one-on-one time so that you will not be interrupted. Before you start, take a time-out to get your emotions under control. During your conversation, use resources if you need to have more information on hand that you do not readily know. Be prepared to talk and answer questions, although it is okay not to have all of the answers. A simple "I don't know, but I'll find out" will keep the lines of communication open. Do not allow your child to ignore the facts as if she has a choice in the matter. Clearly state where her choices are and where there are no choices.

An example of a need-to-know lecture is when your seventeen-year-old daughter comes to you saying that all of her friends are on the birth-control pill. She is going to need to know what it means to go on the Pill—it is so much more than taking a little pill every day. She will need to know the ins and outs of women's health, what a gynecological appointment is like, and so on. She will need to know that while she has a choice whether to have sex, she does not have a choice about whether she takes care of herself medically.

ALERT!

Do not let your opinion keep you from giving your child the information he needs to know to make his choices. The less he knows, the more apt he is to make the wrong choices.

I-Messages

I-messages are a positive way to communicate difficult feelings or communicate about difficult situations. I-messages help ease tension and conflict, reduce defensiveness, assist in defining the problem, and foster honest communication. They are ideal to use when you are in the middle of a stressful confrontation, when you need to give criticism, or when you need to prevent a potentially tense interaction.

There are three parts to an I-message. You start with "I feel . . ." and then add how you feel, describe the problem behavior, and why the behavior was a problem. You can follow I-messages with choices of actions or consequences. For example: "I feel worried when you are late for your curfew because something bad may have happened."

Agree to Disagree with Your Child

By using I-messages you will be able to come to the heart of a problem that you and your child are facing. And you may have to agree to disagree for a solution. It's inevitable. Your child will make choices that you do not agree with. How she spends her money, her choice of friends, and how she feels about politics are just a few areas about which she may have different opinions. The solutions to these types of problems are mutual respect and understanding. By agreeing to disagree, you are telling your child that while you do not agree with her opinion, you still respect and care for her.

Your Parenting Tone

Every parent has a tone that conveys to your child that you are being loving but firm. You are able to use this tone when you are calm and feel strongly about what you are communicating. You are not, however, capable of using this tone when you are overwhelmed, tired, or angry. When you try to use this tone at those times, you will sound mean instead of authoritative. Consequently, whatever message you are communicating will be lost.

Your parenting tone is a useful tool when used correctly. If you find that you are at a point of frustration with your child and you are not capable of using this tone, take a time-out and then give it a try. Do your best not to fall into a yelling and screaming mode. These methods simply do not work as forms of communication with your child. Yelling can even cause fear, which will close the lines of communication.

The Natural Progression of Communication

Your child is capable of communicating his basic needs right from day one. As time marches on, he gradually learns more about communicating his wants and needs to you and others. This is the natural progress of communication.

Birth to Age Two

Most newborn to three-month-old babies can distinguish between pitch and volume of sound. Cooing and making soft noises will get your newborn's attention and help her feel secure. You can never talk too much to children in this age group. As they begin to notice the different things that you are doing, verbalize the actions. "Let's change your diaper" and "Mommy is turning out the light" may seem silly to say to a baby, but she loves to hear the sound of your voice. She will communicate with you by her actions—crying, smiling, and babbling. As infants come close to the age of one, they will be able to imitate expressions, associate simple gestures with words such as waving and saying hi, and respond to a firm "no."

When your child gets closer to the age of two, she may begin to think that her name is "no," and you may also think that it is the only word left in your vocabulary. That's perfectly normal. Children in this age range can say six to twenty words, but they understand many more. They start learning simple phrases and respond correctly to simple questions, such as "What?"

Ages Three to Five

Between the ages of three and five, quite a bit of language development occurs. Children go from joining similar words to make phrases to being able to retell a story. At age three, your child will be able to follow a series of two to four related directions, and he will be able to sing a song and repeat a line or two of his favorite story.

At the ages of four and five, your child will be able to retell a story, but she may confuse the order. She will combine different thoughts into one sentence, listen to long stories, and be able to follow a more complex set of directions. She will be able to use "because" and "so" casually in a conversation and begin to use words like "might," "should," and "can."

Ages Six to Nine

Kids in this age group love to regale you with their stories. They have active imaginations and the capability of adding drama through action and expression. They like to laugh and make others laugh; therefore, jokes become a favorite form of entertainment. Their vocabulary grows as their reading skills improve. Before you know it, you may have to start looking up words in the dictionary in order to converse with them!

 FACT

About 5 percent of school-age children have speech and language disorders, including voice disorders and stuttering. These disorders are handled through speech therapy often provided by the public school system.

Ages Ten to Twelve

Kids in this age group are capable of learning the art of conversation. They have enough knowledge about the world around them and the vocabulary to enjoy a good conversation with you that isn't about when they need to complete their chores. Dinnertime is an excellent opportunity to enjoy such talks. You can start them out with "What did you learn today?"

 ALERT!

Never talk back to your child. There is no room for a snipping and yelling match between parent and child. Although the frustration of dealing with a child who is talking back can become overwhelming, remember that you are the adult.

Children in this age group tend to have problems with back talk. While this may drive you crazy, know that there are reasons behind this behavior. Back talk happens when your child is having strong emotions that he isn't able to express in an appropriate manner. To dissuade back talk, wait until your child is calm and come up with a plan together. Use I-messages to tell your child

how his back talk makes you feel and then ask him what he thinks
he could do instead of talking back to you. Offer suggestions and
then agree on a solution.

Ages Thirteen to Seventeen

Teenagers are capable of having adult-like conversations,
although they will want to have them with their friends instead of
with you. You may at some point feel as if you need to stand on
your head to get more than two words out of them. This is part
of the normal adolescent life stage. But don't stop trying. Keep
those lines of communication open and remain available to them
for when they need to talk to you. They will, and it will be when
you least expect it.

While conversations about tough issues can happen at any time
in your child's life, as children in this age group near adulthood,
they are more frequent. The single, best piece of advice is to prepare yourself long before having any of these conversations. Know
that you are not alone in the situation. Many parents have gone
through and will go through the same type of conversations you are
having. This is the age where not-quite-children-anymore and not-
quite-adults make dire mistakes in judgment. It's normal behavior to
do this. Keep the lines of communication open. That is the single
most important thing you need to do for them at this time.

CHAPTER 13

Discipline

DISCIPLINE IS NOT ABOUT PUNISHMENT. It is about teaching children appropriate behavior by setting guidelines and boundaries. When parents learn to set reasonable expectations and use positive discipline methods as a parenting tool, their children gain security, self-esteem, and self-discipline.

Children Need Discipline

One of the biggest challenges in raising children is providing proper discipline. Part of the reason is that many parents were brought up to believe discipline meant punishment. Consequences are a small part of positive discipline. Many times, in fact, consequences developed by the parent aren't necessary, because other consequences occur naturally.

If parents provide discipline correctly, children will gain security in their boundaries. They will not have to guess at what they can and cannot do. With this security, they will be better able to accomplish goals and build their self-esteem. As they do so, they will learn self-discipline and repeat the cycle, gaining even more security.

Effective Discipline Techniques

You will need to tweak discipline techniques to fit your family's uniqueness. You may even have to tweak each technique for each child, as all children are different. Have patience and try another approach if one doesn't work.

 FACT

Children who are not disciplined—who do not have boundaries and limits—are not able to grow up with high self-esteem. They are more dependent and feel that they have less control over their world. Confidence can only be felt when a child feels in control.

Giving and Taking Time-Outs

Time-outs are used to defuse emotional outbursts and give the person time to think about her behavior and how to change it. They are most effective when the person who is taking the time-out knows what she needs to accomplish during that period of time. Explaining long before a time-out is needed what it is and what is expected to happen during the event establishes this groundwork. Do not begin using time-outs without first explaining them.

Many times parents forget to regulate their own behavior and take a time-out themselves. If you find yourself being rude to your children, yelling, or engaging in any other undesirable behavior, give yourself five minutes. Take a break and relax. It actually is enjoyable.

 ESSENTIAL

The length of a time-out depends on the age of the child. Usually one minute for each year of age, up to five minutes, works. If you need more, give another time-out.

Counting

Many times parents will count. This method is used when a child is displaying inappropriate behavior and the behavior needs to stop. In a calm voice, you begin to count by saying "one." After you say each number, wait a moment to see if the behavior changes to a more appropriate one. You do not continue speaking. You do not threaten in-between numbers. You simply wait to see if the behavior changes. If it does, great! If not, then a consequence happens. The consequence needs to be set beforehand so that your child knows what is coming when you are counting. Generally a time-out works well as a consequence.

Picking Your Battles

There are going to be times when your child's behavior just goes haywire. Everything seems to be wrong. These times may have a precursor, such as the death of a pet. Children will tend to act out in behavior when they are having a hard time dealing with strong emotions like grief. Or your child may simply be hitting puberty and her hormones are running rampant. Whatever the reason, you'll need to choose which behaviors you need to help your child fix and which you will let slide; she is not capable of changing them all at the same time. You'll need to pick your battles, so you can all win the war.

 ALERT!

> Remember to praise your child when she shows the appropriate behavior. Any appropriate behavior can be praised. Praise boosts self-esteem. When you boost their self-esteem, children strive to do better.

Choosing which behaviors to fix first can be a challenge. Start with safety concerns and then work your way through your priorities. Tell your child that from this moment on, he's got a clean slate. Verbalize the behavior that you want to see changed from that moment forward and what the consequence will be if the behavior does not change. Then follow through. Do not comment on the other poor behaviors that need to be changed while you are working on this one, even if it takes weeks. As you step through each behavior, you will find it gets easier and takes him less time to catch on.

Responsibilities and Privileges

As your child grows, he will be given more privileges. Permission to go to friends' houses, later curfews, and going out on his own are things your child will ask for. These are privileges. The smart parent will attach an expectation of a completed responsibility to each privilege when it is asked for. For example, a seven-year-old who wants to be able to play with friends outside is capable of making her bed daily. You'll need to tell her that this is the expectation and if she meets it she has the privilege of playing with friends. The next time she asks to go outside and play with her friends, ask her if her bed is made. If she says yes, then say "Certainly! Have a good time." If her bed is not made, give her the opportunity to complete the task before she receives the privilege.

If you have a hard time thinking of a responsibility to go with a privilege, ask your child for her opinion. Kids often come up with great suggestions that you haven't thought about. You'll have to consider their suggestions carefully to decide whether they are capable of completing the task, as they may set their own expectations too high.

Behavior Modification

Behavior modification is complex. It involves identifying an unwanted behavior that needs to be changed. So you set about changing the behavior to one that is more appropriate. Simply, it's replacing a bad behavior with a good one. But behavior modification is normally not that simple because it is generally used when there is more than one behavior to change.

For example, an eight-year-old who has been recently diagnosed with attention deficit hyperactivity disorder (ADHD) will not begin to act like a perfect angel the minute his medication kicks in. He has spent eight years learning bad habits that need to be modified. With the support of his parents, his behavior modification can work. The parents will need to come up with a plan that slowly changes each of his bad behaviors.

Setting Reasonable Expectations

Simply put, expectations are the behavior you expect from your child. When you set an expectation for your child, communicate it clearly and ask if she understands what you are expecting from her. It is a good idea to ask her to repeat what she thinks she heard, so that you know that she really understood what you expect. It is also a good way to get her to ask you to clarify any points she is having a hard time understanding. When she verbalizes what she thinks you said, questions tend to pop up.

Setting clear expectations can be that easy. Problems start when parents don't follow through by having their child verbalize the expectations and then clarifying the small points. Take, for instance, if you ask your teenage son to take out the trash. You expect that he will take it out. And if you're like many parents, you will expect that he take it out now. He, on the other hand, may have a different view of when it needs to be taken out—like after the football game on television is over. He figures the trash man isn't coming until tomorrow morning, so why jump up now? This will likely lead to a conflict, which is unfortunate because if you had gone just one step further and had him verbalize what he thought was expected, you could have realized he thought you meant "anytime tonight" and clarified that you, in fact, meant "now."

So how do you know if your expectations are reasonable? Here is a list of questions you can ask yourself to see if you're setting reasonable expectations:

- Is your child physically capable of handling the expectation?
- Is your child developmentally capable of understanding the expectation?
- Is your child developmentally capable of completing the expectation?
- What is the reason for the expectation? How does it benefit your child?
- Do you have the time to appreciate your child fully when the expectations are met?

 ESSENTIAL

Many times the expectations that parents set are too high. If you think this may be a problem with one of your expectations, try breaking it down into smaller steps that are part of a greater goal and see if your child responds to those.

There are times when expectations fit all of the criteria, but because of the time it takes to complete the expectation, it is difficult to do it well. You may see this with grades in school. Many times, parents set their expectations by the grades on the report cards. By setting your expectations this way, you will fail to recognize the achievements your child accomplishes throughout the nine weeks of trying to meet that expectation. She will in turn have a much harder time consistently meeting your expectation and when the report card comes, BAM! The grades aren't as good as you both had hoped. If this is happening, break the expectation down to smaller ones. Instead of expecting your child to get Bs or better on her report card, set your goal at doing forty-five minutes of homework each night and a separate goal of sharing all of her work with you. This way you will be able to praise accomplishments and discuss any problems as they are happening.

Reassess your expectations often. Things change and people are unique. Situations will not always be the same; therefore, you need to be able to change your expectations. You're not going to set the same curfew for Saturday night at the movies that you do for the prom. So expect that your teen will come home later on this special occasion and set a later curfew. You're not going to expect your son, who wants to be a carpenter, to get the same grades in science as your daughter, who is studying to be a doctor one day. So when your son brings home a C in science and your daughter gets an A, congratulate both of them.

Natural and Logical Consequences

Logical consequences are situations engineered by the parent, which are logically connected to the wrongdoing. These consequences are logical because they "fit" the offense. For example, if your teen breaks curfew, she is not allowed to go out the next night. If he doesn't eat dinner, then he doesn't get dessert. If she won't turn the music down, she loses the stereo.

Logical consequences are much more effective than "grounding," because they teach reality to your teenager. The punishment fits the crime, which is much like how the real world works. If you don't show up for work, you don't get paid. If you go over the speed limit, you get a fine.

Natural consequences are situations that are not controlled by anyone—they happen naturally. If you put your hand on a hot stove, you get burned. When there is a natural consequence, there is no need to add to it with a logical consequence. There are times, however, when you will need to step in with logical consequences in order for your children to not have to face the natural consequences. For example, if your child runs out into the street without looking, getting hit by a car is the natural consequence. Since this is not an acceptable natural consequence, you will have to use the logical consequence of restricting his privilege of going across the street to see his friend.

Why Spanking Doesn't Work

Spanking as a consequence is based on the fear of getting hurt. Hitting hurts. There is nothing positive about it. Parents who spank have been conditioned to do so by their parents who spanked. It's a bad habit and one that can be broken by replacing it with a more appropriate form of discipline.

There are times, however, where it may be appropriate to cause a little bit of pain. That is when the natural consequence could be death or extreme pain, and your child is not developmentally capable of understanding that. If you catch your toddler ready to place his finger in an electric socket, slapping his hand once will give him the indication that his action causes pain, and it is a lot less painful than the natural consequence.

Power Struggles

Power struggles arise when your preteen tries to assert her independence from you, and you have to lay down the law about what is expected of her. A struggle between the polar opposites ensues, and many times it ends in hurt feelings for both the child and parent. Power struggles tend to come as a shock to parents who are raising their first preteen, but they are a normal developmental behavior. To defuse a power struggle, you need to set reasonable expectations, communicate them clearly, stand firmly behind them, and then walk away. Don't allow yourself to be engaged in the power struggle.

Don't Complicate Matters

If you are too frustrated to discipline your child in a calm manner, then don't discipline your child. Wait until you are calm and thinking rationally, or you are apt to yell or to say something you will later regret. When you complicate your discipline with your frustrations, no one wins. When you get in the habit of disciplining in this fashion, you break down your child's self-esteem. Use your emotional intelligence and take a time-out for yourself.

When Discipline Doesn't Work

Many times, emotional, physical, and mental problems are expressed in behaviors that normally aren't thought of as symptoms of a bigger problem. For instance, a bipolar child may have the symptom of pressured speech, which means he feels the need to talk all of the time. The parents receive calls from the school and try every appropriate discipline technique under the sun to no avail. The discipline isn't working. If this sounds like your situation, you need to take a step back and look at the broader picture. Then you need to take that broader picture to someone who can point you in the right direction.

The broader picture is a combination of other little things that may be going on. Write it all down. Anything about his behaviors that seems a little off, write down. Take it all to his pediatrician and get him a physical. Share your concerns and ask for recommendations. Call the school and ask for more recommendations. While you are checking out this route, there is no need for further discipline.

 **FACT**

Children do not misbehave or fail in school just to get attention. Behavior problems can be symptoms of emotional, behavioral, or mental disorders, rather than merely attention-seeking devices. According to the U.S. Department of Health and Human Services, children's emotional, behavioral, and mental disorders affect millions of American families. An estimated 14 to 20 percent of all children have some type of mental health problem.

The Natural Progression of Discipline

Discipline changes with the development of children as they age. They become capable of more responsibilities and privileges, and they can understand the reasoning behind the rules. The goal as they grow is to teach them how to self-discipline.

Birth to Age Two

You cannot spoil a newborn infant. If your under-a-month-old baby is crying, something is wrong. She is hungry, wet, or uncomfortable. Newborns who wake you up in the middle of the night do not need discipline. They need to be fed, changed, or held. As she grows, you can allow her to cry for a five- to ten-minute span and see if she calms herself. If she does not, check to see if she needs to be changed or is uncomfortable.

Toddlers are capable of understanding time-outs, and you will need to use them quite often during the terrible twos. Pick a place for time-outs such as a corner in the room you are in. They should remain in eyesight at this age for safety reasons. They will also begin to understand natural consequences as they begin to explore their world and tend to get a few bumps and bruises. Comfort them when this happens.

Ages Three to Five

Three-year-olds can follow a series of simple directions. They understand that an action has a reaction and therefore do very well with a reward system and a time-out system. Developmentally, they are capable of sharing with assistance, but do not expect them to be able to share on their own. When your child starts heading toward the age of five, he begins to have some understanding of moral reasoning. Therefore, he can understand that he shouldn't take a toy away from his sister because that hurts her feelings. This is a turning point because now when he goes for a time-out, he is capable of reflecting on what behavior put him there and how to change it for the better.

Ages Six to Nine

The six- to nine-year-olds excel when they are given clear rules and expectations. Praise them when they follow a rule and they will beam with joy. They may think about which rules are fair and be somewhat upset if they think a rule is unfair. Ask them how they would make the rule better, and they may surprise you with an answer you agree with.

Getting privileges to be with friends becomes important. Don't forget to attach small responsibilities when you allow them to start doing more independent things. This age group is capable of doing small chores, and they will do them independently if they have a reminder, such as a to-do list or a sticker calendar.

ALERT!

Six- to nine-year-olds get very upset when they do something wrong. They cry and then worry about it for days. Remember to let them off the hook when they have finished their time-out or have paid their consequence by saying something to the effect of "I know you're going to do better next time."

Ages Ten to Twelve

Letting ten- to twelve-year-olds make choices about their limits when appropriate will help them stick to the guidelines given to them. For instance, in place of giving them a chore to do, give them a list of chores that need to be done and let them pick and choose each week which one they would like to do. Try to be fair and consistent with this group. If they are looking to earn a particular privilege, allow them to earn it with responsibilities.

Twelve-year-olds tend to need a little added security as body-image issues begin to surface. They may start to test their limits just to make sure the limits are still there. Remain steadfast in your expectations.

Ages Thirteen to Seventeen

As teenagers begin the journey toward independence, they may knowingly test the rules and limits a little more often than before. Let them have a say in the expectations that are set as they begin to have their own expectations and goals. Use natural and logical consequences and steer away from grounding. For instance, instead of grounding them for a week, take away a particular privilege. Stay rational when they test the limits; use your emotional intelligence and remind yourself that this is part of their developmental stage.

 **FACT**

> As your child becomes a teenager, he will begin to see you as a fallible human being. Not only can he see why things are right and wrong, he's learned to project it onto you. Since you are the stable figure in his life, you are his first target and the one he will aim at the most.

Older teenagers have the ability to set goals and follow through. You will find your role as disciplinarian slowly ebbs away and turns into the role of an adviser. You may need to develop house rules on curfews, having friends over, and the like. While these aren't rules for them, per se, they do make it very clear that just because your teenager is turning into a young adult doesn't mean she has the run of your household.

CHAPTER 14

Protecting Your Successful Child

YOUR CHILD NEEDS YOUR PROTECTION in order to become successful. Whether that protection is from strangers or from themselves, you could be their key to a safe journey in life. The simple rule for safety is "be prepared."

Safety First

Unintentional injury is the leading cause of death among children ages fourteen and under. For every childhood death caused by injury, there are approximately thirty-four hospitalizations, 1,000 emergency department visits, many more visits to private physicians and school nurses, and an even larger number of injuries treated at home. The percentage of nonfatal unintentional injuries that occur in the home also decreases with age.

It's estimated that by taking simple precautions, close to 90 percent of these unintentional injuries can be avoided. According to the CDC, the leading causes of unintentional injuries are fires/burns, drowning, falls, and poisoning. Each type of injury can occur in different parts of your home and each has its own methods of prevention.

Preventing Falls

Falls are the leading cause of injury among children, and more than 100 children ages fourteen and under die and another 2.5 million are treated in emergency rooms for fall-related injuries. Of those children who die, more than half are ages four and under. These injuries occur inside the home, where parents often think their child is the safest, as well as outdoors when their children are at play. Therefore, preventing falls is a priority for parents.

Never leave your baby or toddler alone on a changing table, bed, stroller, or other furniture. Pull furniture away from windows to prevent children from climbing up and leaning or falling against the window screen; the screen will not be able to hold your child's weight. Use safety gates on stairs and in doorways to outside porches. Don't use baby walkers with wheels; there are stationary activity centers available instead.

 **FACT**

In 2000, 5,686 children died from unintentional injuries; approximately 37 percent of these deaths occurred in or around the home. Home injury deaths are caused primarily by fire and burns, suffocation, drowning, choking, falls, poisoning, and firearms. Young children are at the greatest risk from unintentional injuries in the home because it is where they spend most of their time.

For school-age children, inspect playground equipment thoroughly before allowing your child to use it. Report any damage to the appropriate authority. Make sure the equipment is for use by your child's age level. While your child may object, safety has to come first. Remove loose clothing, including drawstrings on hoods, when your child is playing on playground equipment. Have your child take safety precautions when riding a bike. A helmet is a must, and knee and elbow pads can also prevent injuries. Make sure he wears bright clothing and avoids congested traffic areas.

Check your child's bike to make sure it is the correct size and is working properly. Your child should be able to touch the ground while sitting on the bike's seat.

Water Safety

More than half of childhood drownings occur in a child's home pool and one-third at the homes of friends or relatives. Children can drown in a matter of seconds. It typically occurs when a child is left unattended or during a brief lapse in supervision, such as when a parent leaves to answer a phone.

In order to prevent water injuries or drowning, never leave your child unattended in or around the water, even for a few seconds. Do not rely on flotation devices or on the fact that your child has had swimming lessons. But do get your child swimming lessons after the age of four years old. Learn CPR and basic first aid and have emergency numbers easily accessible. If you own a pool, install four-sided isolation fencing that is at least five feet high and equipped with self-closing, self-latching gates. Fencing should completely surround swimming pools or spas and prevent direct access from a house or yard.

A child can drown in as little as one inch of water. Never leave her unattended in a bathtub, even if most of the water is drained. Empty all containers of liquid after use and keep a watch on children while you are using containers of liquid.

Preventing Poisonings

Child poisoning is a hazard that parents often overlook. Common products such as cosmetics, detergents, and medicines can be fatal to young children if they get hold of them. Never leave these items within their reach. Even innocent-looking items like household plants and vitamin supplements can poison a child in less than a minute. Annually, more than 1.1 million unintentional poisonings among children ages five and under are reported to U.S. poison control centers.

You can prevent your child from becoming poisoned by keeping poisonous products out of reach. Storing potentially harmful products out of sight and reach—in cabinets with safety locks—is one of the best ways of preventing poisonings. Throw away old medicines and other potential poisons. Discard old medicines on a regular basis by flushing them down the toilet. Also, keep poisonous plants out of reach. If your child does eat or drink something that *could* be poisonous—even if you think it may not be—call the American Association of Poison Control Centers at their national toll-free hot line ☎(800) 222-1222.

Fire Safety

Fires can be furious and deadly. In 2000, 561 children aged fourteen and under died in fires. Nearly 40,000 are injured each year in fires. Despite a dramatic 56 percent decline in the fire death rate since the National SAFE KIDS Campaign began in 1988, fires remain a leading cause of unintentional injury-related death among children in the United States.

But there are time-tested ways to prevent fire-related injuries. Simply installing smoke alarms on every level of your home and in every sleeping area, for instance, cuts the chances of dying in a home fire in half. Keeping matches, lighters, and other heat sources out of children's reach can help eliminate child-play fires— the leading cause of fire-related death for children five years old and under.

ALERT!

You know that you do your best to keep your kids safe from unintentional injuries. But there are so many things to be careful of, even some you may not be aware of. Therefore, look for more information about these household and other preventable injuries at the National Safe Kids Campaign on the Internet, ☞*www.safekids.org*. Or write to them at National Safe Kids Campaign, 1301 Pennsylvania Ave., NW, Suite 1000, Washington, D.C. 20004.

The Media

According to the Kaiser Family Foundation's report *Kids and Media at the New Millennium* (1999), the average child spends about five and a half hours daily using media, including television, radio, CDs, or the computer. With this much time spent watching television, listening to the radio, and using the computer, including the Internet, parents need to take an interest in the content of these media outlets. While it can be a nightmare trying to keep up with everything your child sees, does, and listens to, it will be scarier if you don't do your best to monitor the media that affects your child.

Television

Television is the most prevalent form of media in your child's life. Its influence can dominate your child's wants and how your child perceives the world. For instance, take a look at your child's toys, her book bags for school, and her clothing. More than half of these things likely have some kind of cartoon character from television on them or are items she wanted because she saw advertisements for them when she was watching her favorite show. Therefore, as parents you need to be involved in monitoring your child's television viewing. You need to watch out for violence, advertising, and sexual content. You need to limit viewing time and offer other fun activities as alternatives.

 **FACT**

According to the American Psychological Association, before kindergarten, the average child sees 5,000 hours of TV, watching more than 4 hours per day. Most children have watched up to 22,000 hours of TV by the time they graduate from high school.

However, television can offer a lot of benefits to children. Viewing television shows together can give your family some time to enjoy each other. Many families develop a pizza-and-movie night for just this purpose. Often television programs will bring up sensitive issues, giving parents a good segue into discussing these issues with their child. Really good television can even teach children important values and life lessons, and educational television can offer your child socialization and learning skills.

The American Academy of Pediatrics has several suggestions for parents: Encourage a careful selection of programs for your child to view, co-view and discuss content with your child, limit the time your child spends in front of the television and never use it as an electronic babysitter, and model these behaviors by making and limiting your own good viewing choices.

The television industry has received quite a bit of harsh criticism after its first attempt to rate television shows so that parents can make informed decisions about what they will allow their child, or themselves, to view. The first set of ratings was very much like those in the film industry, based on a suggested age group instead of on the content of the television program. These guidelines had parents in an uproar; they enticed younger children to want to watch certain shows simply because they were forbidden fruit, very much like an eleven-year-old wants to go to any PG-13-rated movie as opposed to any G-rated movie. Parents wanted ratings based more on content. The television industry, worried about Congress stepping in and regulating them, gave it to them by adding an extra code for violence, indecent language, and sexual content. These ratings, usually displayed in television guides, are located in the upper left-hand corner of the screen at the beginning of a show.

Here are the rating codes from the FCC and their meanings:

- **TV-Y—All Children**—This program is designed to be appropriate for all children.
- **TV-Y7**—Directed to Older Children—This program is designed for children age seven and older.
- **TV-G**—General Audience—Most parents would find this program suitable for all ages.

- **TV-PG**—Parental Guidance Suggested—This program contains material that parents may find unsuitable for younger children.
- **TV-14**—Parents Strongly Cautioned—This program contains some material that many parents would find unsuitable for children less than fourteen years of age.
- **TV-MA**—Mature Audience Only—This program is specifically designed to be viewed by adults and therefore may be unsuitable for children less than seventeen.

 ESSENTIAL

As of 1999, all new television sets over thirteen inches, sold in the United States have to contain a V-chip. If you choose to utilize the V-chip feature, you select a rating level you feel appropriate for your children. The V-chip reads the transmitted ratings code for all programming and denies access to any programming that exceeds your limitations.

Video Games

The interactive computer game craze isn't such a bad thing. It's more educational than just watching television because your child has to think to participate. The problem comes in when you, as a parent, aren't informed enough about which games are appropriate and which are inappropriate. Of course it's hard to know unless you sit and play every game before your child does, which means you have to buy them first. That can get expensive and time-consuming. But many of the games are violent in nature and shouldn't be played by children of any age.

There is good news! Parents now have the Entertainment Software Rating Board (ESRB). This organization has been formed to help parents make these decisions. The Entertainment Software Rating Board (ESRB) is an independent rating system, which was established in September 1994 by the Interactive Digital Software Association (IDSA), the leading trade association for the interactive entertainment software industry. The ESRB is a voluntary rating system developed to give parents and consumers information about the content of video and computer games so that they can make informed purchase and rental decisions. The ESRB rates the games by randomly selecting raters from a pool of demographically diverse individuals. These raters have been trained in the rating system and go through a game frame by frame before setting the rating. (Of course, you should still monitor games in case they go against your personal values.) Definitions of the ratings used by ESRB are as follows:

- **A—Adults Only:** content suitable only for adults.
- **E—Everyone:** content suitable for children ages six and older.
- **EC—Early Childhood:** content suitable for children ages three and older.
- **M—Mature:** content suitable for persons seventeen and older.
- **RP—Rating Pending:** product has been submitted to the ESRB and is awaiting final rating.
- **T—Teen:** content suitable for persons ages thirteen and older.

 FACT

According to a *Screen Digest* March 2003 study, the video game sector is the fastest growing in the entertainment industry and second only to music in profitability. Global sales of video game software are expected to exceed $18 billion in 2003. The prime audience for video games is boys aged seven to fourteen.

Another common problem with video game playing that is often brought up by parents is the amount of time kids spend playing the games. Setting up an action plan (as described in Chapter 15) can avert this problem with your child, thereby avoiding the power struggle. When you set up the plan and use time limits, keep in mind that many games take a certain amount of time to finish. You can also use video games as some one-on-one time by playing them with your child.

The Music Industry

The music industry and its artists have always been about pushing the limits and creative expression. There is absolutely nothing wrong with that. However, while these music artists are pushing their boundaries, they are taking your child along with them. Yes, it's true that your parents didn't like your music either. But what has been changing from that time is the explicit sexual and violent content that is contained in today's popular hits.

In 1990, the U.S. recording industry introduced Parent Advisory labels to identify music containing explicit lyrics, including depictions of violence and sex. For parents, the system has its downside. The labels are voluntary, so parents can't automatically assume that music without a label will be appropriate for all ages. This is a problem in that one song by an artist may be totally acceptable to a parent, but the others contained on the artist's CD are not acceptable at all. Therefore, when your preteen asks for a CD based on a song that you have heard on the radio with her, you will still need to listen to it in full before letting her have it. One good thing is that most music stores will take back a CD that a parent has found objectionable material on.

In September 2000, the U.S. Federal Trade Commission released a report that showed how the music industry, among other media industries, aggressively marketed their product to teenagers. Of the fifty-five music recordings with explicit Parent Advisory labels the FTC examined, all were targeted to children under seventeen. Marketing plans included placing advertising in media that would reach a majority or a substantial percentage of children under seventeen.

These marketing plans included not only the ads, but also articles in teen magazines about artists who produce nothing but CDs with the Parent Advisory label.

 QUESTION?

Can you trust that all potentially offensive CDs will be labeled?
No. Not all music CDs that have violent or sexually explicit material contain a Parent Advisory label. These labels are voluntary, and the artist or production company chooses to use or not use the label.

Teenagers are developing their identity and self-image. They are vulnerable to outside influences that carry negative messages. These influences have an even greater effect when they bother you, their parent, because it is a normal part of your teen's life stage to want to break away from your boundaries. The music industry, along with much of the media industry, is capitalizing on that fact. While you need to keep an open mind and try not to censor all content that influences your teenager, it is more than appropriate not to allow music in your home that is of a violent or sexual nature. Talk to your children about the music they like to listen to. Start when they are young and expose them to different forms of music, including classical, jazz, the blues, country, and so many more. As your child gets older, talk about the issues the music is bringing forward. For fun, let your teenager know when one of their favorite songs is a remake of one of your old favorites.

The Internet

The Internet encompasses the entire world and places everything at your child's fingertips. This relatively new medium is being taught in schools and parents are having to play catch-up to understand even a little bit of what their child knows about it. Children become savvy fairly quickly, because it is fun and a useful resource. Therefore, to be a parent in the new millennium, you'll need to know how to keep your child safe when they are online.

Know the Benefits

The Internet offers vast resources. When you were studying the Civil War in ninth grade American History, wouldn't it have been nice to have the Library of Congress at your fingertips? Your child does at ✐*www.loc.gov*. They can read any newspaper in the world, or learn to make the best paper airplane from the Guinness record holder for time aloft, Ken Blackburn. The list of excellent sites goes on and on.

 ESSENTIAL

> Surf the Internet with your child to find some fun and resourceful sites. Make it a once-a-month routine for your family nights. Remember to search out sites for homework information, monitored interaction with other children their age, and any particular interests your child has.

The Internet also offers eye-opening experiences. Teenagers these days have the opportunity to prove just how small the world we live in is. There are many monitored message boards and online communities of children over the age of thirteen where they get to know children from all over the world. Your child can learn empathy for children who have firsthand experience with war, or how children in France have the same issues with their parents as your child has with you.

Know the Risks

There are risks with Internet usage. But the positive benefits far outweigh the risks especially because the risks can be avoided by following the simple rules of the road. While your child needs to be responsible for following these rules, it is your responsibility to clearly communicate what they are and make sure that they are doing so.

Children, and adults, have the right not to give out private information to anyone, including reputable companies, for any reason without the expressed permission of their parents. This information includes, but is not limited to, name, e-mail, address, age, and school they attend. Read the privacy statements on the Internet sites your child visits. Only allow those that do not require registration in order to use the site.

 **FACT**

According to the report done by National Telecommunications and Information Administration, of those that access the Internet at home, 77.9 percent use it to e-mail; of that group, 93.6 percent use e-mail to communicate with family and friends. E-mail remains the most used application of those with home Internet access.

The Internet is a vast information resource—of all types of information. Sites that contain explicit sexual, violent, and hateful information can be found with little and sometimes no effort. There are also sites on how to build bombs, make designer drugs, and everything else under the sun. If you find your child has come upon one of these sites, do not assume he searched it out, but talk to him about it.

Chat rooms and message boards are chock full of people who are just plain nasty. This can hurt a child's self-esteem. Also, there are those on the Net that will harass via e-mail. A teenager with a credit card can do major damage to their credit, or yours. You should not allow any purchases for anything on the Internet without your permission. Then it should only be done on a secure server and never through e-mail.

Know What to Do

First and foremost when you allow your child to be on the Internet, you need filtering software. Sometimes this software can be obtained through your Internet Service Provider; sometimes you need to purchase a software program. Either way, these programs can protect your child from accidentally, or purposefully, going to sites where they shouldn't be.

Let your teen know it is all right to *not* tell things to people on the Internet. Teach them to protect their privacy, that things aren't always what they seem. Make an action plan with your child (see Chapter 15 for how to do this). This will enable them to know what you expect of their behavior while online. Use the family filters on the major search engines. These can be found under the search engine's advanced search options. Check out your favorite search engine's filtering capabilities before your child uses it.

Obtain a free e-mail account for your child from one of the many services that offer them. These types of accounts keep the spam level down and do not reveal the area in which your child lives, like an e-mail address from a local ISP can.

 ALERT!

You may need to "snoop" in order to keep your child safe. Let your child know that this is possible before you feel the need to take a look and explain to him that it is your responsibility to protect him, even if it is from himself. The risks are too great not to do this.

Report harassment or sexual exploitation. If someone sends you messages or images that are obscene, lewd, filthy, or indecent with the intent to harass, abuse, annoy, or threaten your child, report it to your Internet service provider and the CyberTipline online at *www.missingkids.com* or by calling 1-800-843-5678.

Protecting Children from Themselves

It is a natural tendency for a child to want to do more than is age appropriate. Often, you have to hold them back for their own safety. You will see this at every age level. It is the driving force behind the terrible twos, the reason your eight-year-old daughter wants to wear makeup and an explanation for your fifteen-year-old son's "dire" need for a motorcycle.

You will need to be the force in their lives that decides what is safe for your child to do and what isn't. You will have to set the limits based on these facts and not on how much you wish you could give your child what he wants. You will need to take the responsibility of standing up to the "but everyone else's parents let them do it." Because sometimes that statement is true, even though what everyone else's parents are letting their kids do isn't necessarily the safest option.

Being Prepared Matters

While some believe ignorance is bliss, for a parent, nothing could be further from the truth. The more informed you have about any topic that affects your child, the better off your child will be. You don't need to think that your child is taking drugs before you learn the warning signs of teenage drug abuse. With these in your knowledge base, you will be capable of knowing if your child, or one of your child's friends starts to become involved in drugs before it becomes a real problem for them.

Sometimes preparing for the worst can seem like you're expecting it to happen. Nothing could be farther from the truth. When you prepare and know what could happen, you will gain the confidence it takes to set up roadblocks to preventing the worst from happening. This is successful parenting at its best.

CHAPTER 15

Problem-Solving

PARENTS WITH EFFICIENT PROBLEM-SOLVING skills enjoy a calmer household. They have peace of mind because no matter what comes up, it can be solved. If this doesn't sound like your home, brush up on this problem-solving technique. Keep it handy in your parenting toolbox because you will need to use it daily.

Learning Problem-Solving Skills

When children learn problem-solving skills, they are more self-confident. They have fewer behavior problems and get along better with other people. This enables them to do better in school and in relationships with friends and authority figures. They also tend to have strong emotional health, which gives them the ability to deal with life's challenges and difficult events.

When you learn to coach your child through a problem, instead of solving it for them or ignoring it, you are empowering him to become independent. You are giving him the ability to smooth out life's bumps in the road, and thereby be able to travel farther down it. You are showing him a key tool to success.

Identify the Problem

There are several steps to identifying a problem; the first is to recognize that there *is* a problem. Once that is determined, you need to name the parties who are part of the problem. Often it is one person, but many times there are two or more. After that, you must clearly define the problem you wish to solve.

 FACT

Psychologist Abraham Maslow said about conflict and problem-solving: "If the only tools you have are hammers, every problem begins to look like a nail." There is no truer statement when you are trying to help your child figure out the solution to a problem. Learn the skill and make it unique to your family.

Separating the Issues

Quite often, there is more than one problem in a particular situation, and you must be able to separate them and confront them individually. For example, one child takes a toy from another, and the other child reacts by hitting the first child. In this example you have two problems: the taking of the toy and the hitting of the child. Although you will have to deal right away with calming the child who got hit, you first need to identify the action that caused the ruckus and deal with it. Afterward, you can deal with other problems (such as calming the child who was hit) that developed from the reactions to the initial problem. Begin by asking one child what happened, and give each child a turn in giving her version of the events. Then state that there is a problem that you, as a group, need to solve. State clearly which problem you are solving. In this instance, you are attempting first to solve the problem of the child taking the toy first, and then you will use problem-solving skills to come up with alternatives to hitting another person.

Get to the Root

Coming on a scene where one child is crying sometimes causes parents to put on blinders to everything else that may be going on. Yes, it is extremely important to make sure that the child who is crying is not hurt. Once that is determined, it's time to get to the root problem. If you ignore what caused the scene and don't try to fix the problems that resulted first, you will be teaching the children that you can fix things with bandages instead of teaching them a way to solve the next problem. Therefore, they will continually need you to be there to apply the bandage.

All too often when a problem occurs between two or more children, there isn't an adult in the room. Therefore, identifying the root problem can get tricky. This can lead to another problem: lying. Try to get an account of what happened from one child at a time. If you suspect that a child may not be telling the truth and may make it hard to figure out who to believe, shelve the entire mess. Have everyone, including you, take a group time-out. Once everyone is calm, move on. If you've determined that it's impossible to figure out the problem accurately, trying to find the problem becomes the problem. You never want to guess, because you could be wrong, which will cause guilt and possibly shame in someone who doesn't deserve it. Shelve it, move on, and pay closer attention to the group from here on.

 ALERT!

If it is clear that a child is lying about the situation, you will need to implement a disciplinary action, such as a time-out, before trying to solve the problem. But bring that child back into the group to help with the problem-solving.

Determine the Goal

After you have defined the problem, you must figure out what the best outcome would be; what is the goal? The goal of this problem is that each child is happy. The goal is not that a child gets the toy that is being fought over. With only one toy and two children, that goal would be self-defeating. Therefore, at least one child needs to be happy without the toy for the problem to be solved.

List the Solutions

There are many possible solutions to every problem. You can verbally list them or write them down. Let everyone who is involved in the problem give options that would solve the problem. You may have to help younger children come up with different solutions. Offer them suggestions, but let them choose. Allow them to get creative and give them plenty of time to come up with options.

The most important part of listing solutions is that you allow all of the possibilities. No solution is too stupid, silly, or impractical. If one child in the example feels that leaving and going to Disney World is the solution, then that is a viable option to him and it needs to be respected. Think about your goal. When you tell a child that the goal is for everyone to be happy, Disney World really is an option. Once everyone has given his or her opinion, it's time to choose a solution to try.

 ESSENTIAL

Using a paper and pencil will help you remember all of the options listed when you are ready to choose a solution. You will cause hurt feelings if you forget a solution that a child has come up with. Avoid this by simply writing down all the options mentioned.

Choose a Solution

Evaluate each option as if it is doable, listing the pros and cons for each suggestion. This is a good time to set limits on what is allowable and what is not. For instance, say, one of the children in our ongoing example offered the option of keeping the toy as a possible solution. You listed it because it is a possible solution. But, it is not within the limits of good behavior since it would be a selfish act. Therefore, it is not a solution that the children can try out as an answer to their problem.

Help each child go over each option. You may also have to have the last say about whether an option is viable. If you do, give a reason that it is not a good option to try, but do not get into a power struggle over it. Say no, give the reason, and move on.

Re-evaluate

Did the solution you chose work? Would it have worked better if there were slight changes? Do you need to try another option?

Do not throw away a solution if it doesn't work the first time. Follow through with it again, possibly a couple of more times. Often it just takes everyone getting used to the new solution to this particular problem because they had handled it differently in the past. If, however, the decision doesn't work at all, begin to problem-solve the original problem again.

 ALERT!

Not all solutions work and sometimes they lead to more problems. This is normal. Instead of trying to fix all of the new problems, see if going back to the original problem and choosing another solution will help.

Taking Ownership of the Problem

Often the question is not "what is the problem," but "whose problem is it." Many times, you will take ownership of your child's problems. Using our two children, one toy example: Many parents might have fixed that problem differently. They would zoom into the room, take both children out of the situation, and redirect their interest by offering the children ice cream. The children are happy. The goal is met. The problem is solved. The only glitch here is that they have just taught these two children that by fighting over a toy, they get ice cream. Not to mention the fact that they have missed an opportunity to teach those two children to problem-solve.

In order to become successful, children need to get over life's hurdles. They do not need you to get them over the hurdles. They must learn how to do this on their own. They need to take ownership of their own problems, and it is your job to teach them how.

Don't Become the Problem

If you are not feeling up to the task of helping your child solve a problem correctly, take some time out for yourself before trying to do so. You need to be able to give him your undivided attention so you can help him solve his problem and not become part of it. Much of parenting is putting your emotions aside in order to complete a task. This is never truer than when there is a problem to solve. And if you think about it, that is basically all the time.

Your Limits and Boundaries

Children need limits and boundaries in order to feel secure in their world. However, if your limits are stifling your child's ability to solve a problem, it is time to take a look at them and revamp them. That is not to say that you should drop a limit you have set but perhaps tweaking it some may allow your child to learn a valuable lesson.

Let Your Child Handle "Other People"

Your child may have a problem with someone with whom you have little contact. This often happens with teachers or friends at school. Your child may come home and tell you how unfair the teacher was to give her extra homework because she was talking in math class. Or, a friend didn't want to be her friend that day. Commiserate with her, share a similar experience you've had, and help her solve her problem—but allow her to handle it. If you go to bat for your child with other people, she will expect you to do that all of the time and will never learn to handle the other people in her life.

 **FACT**

One of the most common complaints teachers have is that parents are not involved enough. Initiate a conversation at the beginning of the school year, by calling and introducing yourself or sending a note, so your child's teacher knows you are available if needed.

Take Your Time

As a parent, you will often try to solve problems for your child. Even when you are helping him problem-solve, you may offer answers to the problem instead of suggestions and ask questions when he comes up with suggestions. The thing to keep in mind when teaching and learning problem-solving skills is to take your time. As you turn this skill into a habit, you'll actually save time because your child will begin to be able to solve problems on his own and there will be fewer power struggles when you need to intervene. Solutions to problems will be more readily available to you.

Using an Action Plan

Parent-child contracts, or action plans, are tools in which each party—parent and child—clearly states goals and responsibilities in order to solve or prevent a problem or set of problems. It is often seen as a form of discipline, although that is not totally correct. These contracts can be used very effectively to solve the problem of earning a new privilege. There are, however, consequences clearly defined in the plan.

In a situation where earning a new privilege is the goal, a parent-child contract is a clear-cut, win-win situation plan. Your child lets you know exactly what she wants, the privilege, and you in turn let her know what responsibility she must take on to earn that privilege. Consequences for inappropriate behavior can also be added to the plan. This allows everything to be clearly defined. Then, you write it down and you both sign it. By setting up a problem this way, you empower your child with the ability to solve it. All she has to do to solve her problem of earning a privilege is follow the plan. If she completes the responsibility, she gets the privilege. If she does not complete the responsibility, she can try again. You are empowering her with this ability through the plan. She is learning to problem-solve successfully on her own.

In order to create an effective contract, all parties that the plan affects need to be included in the discussion. The plan should begin with a statement about what the privilege is and why it is worth having. This will help you and your child remember why the privilege is worth earning.

Next, lay out the rules required in order to gain the privilege. Problem-solve all aspects of the privilege. Basically in this section, you're laying down the law. Include the consequences should any of the rules in the plan be broken. Finally, all parties must sign the plan at the end. See the sample contract on page 175.

The Natural Progression of Problem-Solving

Problem-solving is most often learned through trial and error, as opposed to observational learning. Because of this, it can be very hard to sit back and watch your child learn problem-solving skills. No parent likes to watch his child fail. It is advantageous, however, to let him. He will learn what it feels like to fail and learn how to try again. Through this process, he will eventually learn what it is like to succeed on his own—a very good feeling indeed.

As your child grows, you will also experience some trial-and-error learning when you try to decide what problems to let him handle and what problems to help him with. You can gauge this by allowing him to try new things, observing how he handles any

I know that the Internet is not a toy. It is as interesting, and as dangerous, as being able to walk down any street, in any town or city, in the world. It reflects all parts of life today, which is fascinating and scary.

In order to have the privilege of using the Internet, I need to follow these rules, so I can earn the privilege of using the Internet and keep my family and myself safe.

1. I will take the household trash out to the curb every Wednesday night before 7 P.M.
2. I will never give out personal information to anyone online, including, but not limited to, my full name, my address, my passwords, and my phone number.
3. I will always be polite when chatting online. I will treat people with the respect that I expect to be given. If I am treated unkindly, I will not reciprocate in the same manner. I will leave the chat room if I get too angry.
4. I will never personally meet anyone I have met online without the permission of my parents. If this opportunity should arise, I fully expect my parents to come to the meeting.
5. I will never call anyone I have met online without the permission of my parents.
6. I will report all incidents in chat rooms to my parents and to the room administrators.
7. I will not go surfing in areas that are not appropriate, including, but not limited to, Web sites that are of a sexual nature, that promote hate, that are offensive in language, and that are of a violent nature.
8. I will not go surfing around looking for new places without my parents' permission.
9. I will follow these rules whether I am at home, at school, or at a friend's home. If my friend is not following these rules, I will leave.
10. I will not purchase anything online without the permission of my parents.

If I do not follow these rules, I know that I will lose computer privileges for one full week.

Signature: _____

Parent's Signature:_____

conflicts that arise, and stepping in should he become too discouraged to continue. Always be encouraging when your child is handling a problem by guiding him, but still allowing him to do the solving.

Birth to Age Two

Babies are born with one simple solution to problem-solving. They cry for you and then you solve their problem. One-year-olds need to be redirected. Say the problem and solution out loud while you are redirecting them so that they begin to recognize actions and reactions.

As they near the age of two, start showing them how to solve their own problems by following all of the steps. Re-evaluate the problem when it pops up again. With two-year-olds, that will be within the next five minutes. This is a busy time for your child, and a very busy time for you. Around every corner is a problem; don't try to solve them all. You need not go through every step, every single time the same problem comes up; otherwise you may not have time for things like eating and sleeping. Once you go through the steps two or three times, just remind your two- to three-year-old that the solution was found and allow her to show you that she remembers it.

Ages Three to Five

Three- to five-year-olds are capable of learning how to problem-solve by breaking problems down and choosing a solution. You will need to offer suggestions and options for how to solve the problem, since they may only be able to see a single option. Take the time to go through the steps and ask them how they would like to solve the problem. You will still need to redirect them at times, especially when they may do physical harm to themselves or another.

Ages Six to Nine

Children in this age group love solving problems. They find puzzles to be a lot of fun. You may have to show them that there is a problem to begin with, but after that they will go at it full force.

After they solve their problem, they will want to know if they did it right. Be generous with your praise and gentle with any criticism.

Ages Ten to Twelve

Preteens will begin to see the many aspects of each problem they face. Their list of options for solving a problem may be enough to fill a book. Some of those options will be humorous as they begin to see a problem as something to be solved as opposed to something to be afraid of. They will also be very matter-of-fact when solving a problem they have handled before.

Ages Thirteen to Seventeen

The teenage years are all about responsibility and privileges. Parent-child contracts do wonders with this age group. When teenagers are given these win-win situations, they are empowered to help themselves. This gives them not only the freedom they long for, but also the limits they need.

As your children reach for adulthood, they will face problems of a larger magnitude. Teenage pregnancy, drug use, and school violence are life-changing problems that are scary to parents and teenagers. Many times their friends are facing these types of problems. Spend some time with your child to evaluate these problems long before there is an issue with her. Empower her to prevent these problems from happening to her.

CHAPTER 16

Family Traditions

FAMILY TRADITIONS AND RITUALS form a sense of unity for children. They teach tolerance, give a sense of belonging, and are a lot of fun. For parents, they are also a lot of work. But by using your decision-making and organizational skills, you can employ stress-free family traditions as a parenting tool that you will enjoy too.

The Importance of Family Traditions

Cultivating your family rituals and traditions cannot be left to chance. In today's hustle and bustle world, however, many families are doing just that. Activities, sports, work, school, and other commitments can have members of your family running in different directions much of the time. So much so that without you consciously establishing family rituals and traditions your family can lose their sense of unity and become just a group of people living under one roof.

What Makes a Tradition?

Family traditions don't have to cost any money, and they don't have to be elaborate. The main ingredients in a family tradition are fun and togetherness. Saying goodbye with a hug and a kiss ever day before you

walk out the door is a simple family tradition. Opening presents from extended family on Christmas Eve is a simple family tradition.

Traditions need to be fun and need to repeat themselves normally on a set schedule. For instance, you kiss your children good night daily, you have a large spaghetti dinner weekly, or you celebrate a holiday yearly. Repetition is what makes a fun event into a tradition.

ALERT!

While you can coordinate the family traditions, you should not try to handle everything on your own. Delegate some of the responsibility to each family member. Even the youngest can handle a small amount of responsibility.

When an event repeats itself in a family, children begin anticipating it. They will expect it to happen on its schedule. They will participate and then reflect on the memories. For instance, if you begin to let your child choose the dinner menu on her birthday, the next year, she will begin to plan what she wants for her birthday dinner long before it's her birthday. She may even take ownership and boast about how good her dinner was and how she can't wait until next year.

A Sense of Belonging

Family traditions provide time and space for you to be together as a family. This is a time to affirm family values, strengthen family ties, and enjoy each other's company. When you make the time to spend together as a family, your child gets a sense of belonging. He begins to understand that he fits in with this group of people.

When you celebrate your family's traditional holidays with extended family, your child comes to realize that he is part of a larger group of people. He gets a sense of family unity. He gains strength from knowing that he is part of the larger family unit.

He may hear stories about other family occasions, events, and members that either he is too young to remember or that happened before he was born. He will gain a sense of continuity from these celebrations. He will learn to carry on his family traditions.

All of this will help him with his identity. He will have a start to answering questions about who he is that spring up during adolescence. Family traditions can also help with the bumps in the road of adolescence, because they strengthen families in good times and in bad.

Teaching Tolerance

Many times when people talk about the differences in cultures and religions, they use family traditions and rituals as examples. For example, a Christian family may explain to their children that Jewish families celebrate Hanukkah around Christmas-time. Although this is a simplistic explanation, for young children this is more appropriate than explaining the entire theology of different religions.

 **FACT**

Tolerance or intolerance is learned from the family. Your child will model your behavior when dealing with exposure to different cultures or religions. It is important in this multicultural world to take some time out and teach your children tolerance for things that are different from what they have experienced.

If you take this explanation one step further, however, you will be able to teach your child tolerance of cultures and religions other than her own. First, explain a little about the difference between the culture or religion and your own. Try not to be too complicated; simple is best. Then point to your tradition and ask your child how she feels about it. How would she feel if she couldn't celebrate it? Explain how much you enjoy celebrating the tradition with her and how sad you would be if you couldn't. Tell her how it makes you feel closer to her. Then, turn the tables and say the same thing about the other family's tradition. Explain how sad they would feel if they couldn't celebrate something that makes them feel closer. She doesn't need to totally understand the other culture. Instead, by tapping into your child's feelings about something she already knows, she can understand how the other family feels, and the result is tolerance.

Fun! Fun! Fun!

How do you create family rituals and traditions that are fun and rewarding? You start by not getting caught up in making them perfect. No one will have any fun if you are too worried about everyone enjoying the ritual.

Daily Rituals

For daily rituals, incorporate hugs, hellos, and goodbyes into your day. Make it a point to always hug and kiss your children when they get up in the morning. If they become uncomfortable with this when they get older, try a high-five or a pat on the back. Never let your child go to bed without a good night from you.

Dinnertime is the perfect time to start a daily ritual. Talking about the day's events over the evening meal is meaningful to your child.

Weekly Routines

Weekly rituals include attending youth organization meetings or sporting events that your child is a part of and enjoying those as a family. However, remember that every family ritual does not have to include the entire family. If you coach your son's little league and you have games on Saturday morning, this is a weekly family ritual for the baseball season. Although it is nice if the whole family can attend the game, if some are unable to go because of other commitments, there is no need to force the issue. Do not turn family rituals into power struggles.

Annual Events

For yearly or seasonal traditions, go with your family's flow. Try some new activities or visit a new place. If everyone enjoys it, make plans to go again the following year. You can make doing something new or going someplace different a family tradition. If you try this, allow the whole family to have input on where to go and what to do.

Holidays, birthdays, and other special occasions should incorporate yearly family traditions. Simple family rituals for these days are as important as the big traditional celebrations. Letting your child choose the meal for his birthday dinner, opening one gift on Christmas Eve, or taking a family picture every spring are all unique to your family and will be special to your children.

Making Your House a Home

By using daily, weekly, monthly, and yearly family traditions, you turn your house, the roof you live under, into a home, a place where your family feels love, security, and unity. Think about how nice it is for a child to come home from school, see a snack ready for her on the table, and your smiling face waiting to ask how her day went, every single day. Or, if you work, leave him a note telling him that you love him and that you are looking forward to seeing him when you get home that evening. He will feel secure that you are there for him. He will know that you love him because you told him and showed him.

 ESSENTIAL

Setting up specific dates and times helps a child establish a routine when he needs to get a daily or weekly task done. If you incorporate the entire family into the task, as with chores, it becomes a family ritual.

Dinnertime should be family time, not just a time when you eat. Sit down and enjoy one another's company. If this is hard because of a busy evening schedule, you may need to change the schedule. Bring up conversations by asking questions about your child's day. You will find that she will model this behavior and start asking you too.

Religious Beliefs

Attending religious services weekly is a common family tradition. Parents need to give their children a religious identity. Most children want this from them. When your child can relate an event in his daily life to his religious beliefs, it strengthens his ties to church and to family. Even young children can benefit from being a part of their religious community. Again, they will gain a sense of belonging to something bigger than they are, which will give them security.

Problems tend to come up when both parents do not share the same religious background. Families handle this in a variety of fashions. Some families decide to blend the religions or split their religious traditions, choosing some aspects of one and some from the other; others choose one over the other. Either decision is correct as long as you make a conscious effort to make it work for the family, as a unit. Otherwise, you destroy one of the reasons to follow through with this family tradition—family unity.

Holiday Whirlwinds

The holidays can often be a stressful time for parents. It's basically because you're in charge; therefore, you have all of the responsibility of getting everything done in order for everyone to have a good time. In this way, holidays and special occasions become whirlwinds for parents. Never fear, there are ways to organize holidays so that you get to enjoy them as much as everyone else.

When you became a family, you gained the right to pick and choose your own family traditions. There is no reason you have to follow along with what your family did or what your partner's family did. You do not have to choose one way or the other. You can make your own way.

Both sets of extended family will want some of your time, which is okay. But when to see them and how much time you spend with them needs to be set by you. For example, some families spend Christmas morning opening presents at home and split Christmas Eve and Christmas afternoon between their families. Or, if your family doesn't live locally, you can switch from year to year. You could also offer to host the occasion in your home. Whatever option you choose, try to remain fair to everyone while putting your family's needs first.

This may at some point cause frustration for you or your partner's families. They may in turn do or say something that will cause you to feel some guilt. Do not change your mind because of this guilt. Take a second look at what you are doing. If you have remained as fair as possible while keeping your family's needs first, drop the guilt. A simple "I'm sorry you feel that way, but this is what we feel is best for our family" will have to do.

One-on-One Time

Having special one-on-one time is an excellent family tradition. This is especially important if you have more than one child, but it is also important for each parent to have time with a child, even when there is only one. One-on-one time is time you spend with your child alone, without any other siblings or your spouse. As you spend this time together, you learn about each other's personality away from the daily routines of family life.

Parents who make the time to spend with their child in a one-to-one setting find that the lines of communication remain open as the child gets older. When your child knows that there is a set time when she will have your complete undivided attention, she will feel more secure. If she is always vying for your attention, she may act out or begin to not communicate with you at all.

While not every outing will be a revelation, it does give your child the opportunity to bring up tough issues with you without enduring the embarrassment of the entire family knowing what is going on. For example, say, your fifth-grade daughter has "the talk" in school about puberty. She is more apt to talk with you about it during a time that she is used to being with you when she already feels very comfortable, than if you make the time to talk to her about just that. She'll be less embarrassed because her siblings won't be asking why the two of you need to talk. She'll feel secure because she knows that you are there for her and for her alone.

Setting a Budget for Traditions

Nothing causes more stress around the holidays or other family events as the budget. Much of the time the stress is due to the fact that there is no budget. A budget is not just an amount of money that you grab and think this is all you can spend. Keeping a budget for the expenses of family traditions is as important as setting the date and time. You need to sit down long before Christmas or your family vacation and actually figure out how much money you will have to spend on what. Then you need to put that money aside and track its use. If you do this, you will carry a lot less stress over the occasion.

 **FACT**

One of the reasons cited for families not vacationing together is that they are unable to financially. You will find, though, that with just a little planning, you may be able to take a vacation after all. A vacation doesn't have to be anything exotic, faraway, or expensive. Consider a few days away in a nearby area, for example. The important thing is to have a "break" from your normal routine and spend some time together as a family.

For example, here is how to budget for a family vacation. If you like to go to the same vacation spot year after year, this is very easy. If not, you'll need to do some guesswork. First, tally up all of the expenses you had on your last vacation. Don't forget gas, hotel, food, and all activities. Estimate high if you do not have exact figures. Next add 10 percent of that figure. So if last year's vacation cost you $1,000, your estimate for next year's vacation is $1,100.

Divide that figure by fifty-two, if you get paid weekly, or by twenty-six, if you get paid biweekly. Then every time you get paid, place that amount of money in a special vacation fund or plan that you set up at your bank—it can be as simple as a second savings account—so you won't touch it. Don't have every good intention of doing this and then not do it. Do it right away. Start today, even if part of the year has gone by already. The more you save now, the less anxiety you will have a month before you want to go and you begin to worry about how much it will cost. There will be no need to worry, because you have put the money aside and you can enjoy the anticipation of the family vacation with your children. After all, that is what family traditions are all about. It isn't just about giving your child a good time. It's about enjoying each other.

 ALERT!

Do not let your child take over the entire responsibility of budgeting for your family outings. If she fails, everyone will suffer. Set up a win-win situation where you continue to do some checks and balances.

As your child gets older, you can have him help with setting and tracking a budget. Give him a spreadsheet, either on the computer or on a piece of paper. Explain the expenses and how much you will need for next year's vacation. Every time you deposit an amount into your fund, have him add it in. He can even create a monthly report on your budget. Because he is looking forward to going on the vacation, this is an excellent way for him to learn budgeting.

The Natural Progression of Family Traditions

Family rituals and traditions are important from the get-go, even before you have children. This parenting tool brings unity to a family, helps family members feel secure, and gives them a sense of belonging. Your identity as a family will be strengthened, and therefore, your child will be better able to answer the questions about who she is and where she belongs that come up in childhood and remain through adulthood. Family traditions will bring happiness and joy into your child's life, a key trait in success.

Birth to Age Two

As an infant, your child will not know the difference between being on vacation and being at home. He will just enjoy being in your arms in either situation. But you do know the difference, so this is a good time to start planning out some of yearly events that you want to make into traditions. Your hardest task will likely be splitting up the holidays between extended family because everyone will want to have time with the baby.

You set the stage at this age for daily routines. Wake him up with a smile, a hug, and a good morning. Spend some quiet time before bed reading a book and tucking him in. While your two-year-old is not yet ready for family discussions at the dinner table, a set dinnertime will help get him ready for it.

Ages Three to Five

Children at this age are so creative, and they love anticipating an event. Allow them to give input to your yearly traditions. Have some fun anticipating an event with them and share in their excitement.

The comfort of a daily ritual will help this age child begin exploring the world around her without you. When your child knows she will get up in the morning to a smile and a hug, she will sleep peacefully when you say, "See you in the morning." Start incorporating discussions at dinnertime. Keep up with a nighttime routine that allows her some quiet time.

Ages Six to Nine

Children this age love to plan as well as do. Allow them to pick a family outing by giving them a few choices of where to go. Make their birthdays special by allowing them to choose the meal or type of cake. Let them have a calendar to mark special days. They will love to cross off the days as they anticipate the event.

Daily family rituals are very important at this age. Children will come to expect the routine and will let you know if you veer off the normal path. This is because your child is protecting his security. The family, with its routines and rituals, is his foundation as he explores his new world in school and with new friendships. Try to keep your morning and nighttime rituals the same every day. Life is getting busier for your child, who now has homework and other obligations. Therefore, your family rituals are even more important.

This is also a good time to start new family traditions that involve responsibility. Weekly chores work very well at this age. A set time to get something done such as cleaning his room will help him complete the task without a power struggle.

Ages Ten to Twelve

As your child reaches the preteen years, she can take on more of the responsibility of yearly rituals. Packing her own suitcase for vacations or earning money through chores for Christmas gifts is a good way to begin showing her the responsibilities that come with having fun. Preteens may begin to seem uninterested in your weekly or daily family traditions. This is the start of teenage angst and may be due to growing pains. This is all the more reason to keep up with your family rituals and traditions. By keeping up with the routines, even when your child is fighting them, you will strengthen her sense of belonging.

Ages Thirteen to Seventeen

Teenagers need to own part of their family traditions. They may have other wants and needs than the rest of the family; therefore, allow your teen to give input when planning where the next family vacation will be, what you are doing on their birthday, or how to spend the holidays. Verbalize your plans with him or you may be surprised to find out that he has made other plans with friends. You may at times need to remind him that family is important too, and he needs to fit some time in his busy schedule for his family.

 ESSENTIAL

Preteens and teens go through many changes physically and emotionally. They begin growing again almost as quickly as they did when they were babies and toddlers. Try to be patient with their crankiness toward family rituals. It is a stage that will pass.

Rituals that involve communication are a must with children at this age. Keep up with a morning and nighttime routine that shows love and affection, even when times are tough and you aren't happy with your teenager's behavior. Your child will get a sense of knowing that you love him no matter what through these rituals.

CHAPTER 17

Extracurricular Activities

S UCCESSFUL CHILDREN NEED more in life than school and home. They need to be challenged in areas that pique their interests. Help them grow to their potential by supporting the extracurricular activities that they choose.

Start Early and Diversify

There isn't a specific age at which your child should start extracurricular activities. Even babies get together for play dates in moms' clubs across America. Communities offer activities such as "tumble tots" where mothers and two-year-olds go to tumble around a gymnastics mat. Your child can start these activities at any time.

When your child starts a new activity, make sure she is developmentally and physically ready for the task. If your child is on the young end of those children who are signing up for T-ball, for example, you may want to wait another year before she tries that activity. Children who aren't physically capable of handling an activity but are forced to try will not have a good experience. Therefore, they will shy away from other activities that you offer them. By waiting a year, and perhaps trying something else in the meantime, you will ensure that your child will enjoy her experience and have fun—which is what extracurricular activities are all about.

Although it may seem like all the extracurricular activities that are offered in your community or at your child's school are related to team sports, there are other alternatives. Cultural activities are often found at the local library. An art studio or community college may offer art classes. Local Scout troops and YMCA/YWCAs also offer alternative activities. Cooking, sewing, and collecting can all be done in your home. The first and foremost priority for any extracurricular activity is that it piques your child's interest and she enjoys it.

Use Your Child's Interests, Not Yours

You'll need to use what your child likes to do as a guide for choosing activities for him. One trap parents tend to fall into is using what they are interested in doing instead. This could turn your child against doing any types of activities because he will feel forced into the activity that you enjoy. For instance, if you are extremely good at soccer and you would like to see your child enjoy it as well, that is wonderful. But if your son enjoys playing football instead, you will need to let go of that soccer dream without placing guilt on him. It's his turn to work out what his dreams are and choose the activities he enjoys.

 ESSENTIAL

Notice your child's interest by paying attention to what makes her smile and laugh. What does she like to do with her peers? Are there activities she could try with a friend? Sign up for mailing lists that will send you activity calendars from your local community center, the library, or the nearest bowling alley.

Having Too Many Interests

There are children who absolutely love everything they do and try. They have natural athletic talent, are quick witted and able to pick up new things easily, and really enjoy being active. These types of children end up in a dilemma when they need to pick and choose what they want to do as an extracurricular activity because they want to do everything. You will need to help them find their niche. Otherwise, your son or daughter is likely to become overwhelmed with all that is going on and may begin to feel stressed in keeping up with it all.

The impact of stress on a child depends on her personality, maturity, and style of coping. Children often have difficulty describing exactly how they feel. Instead of saying "I feel overwhelmed," they might say, "My stomach hurts." Other signs of stress in some children include crying, displaying aggressive behavior, talking back or acting irritable, or becoming nervous or fearful.

Make a plan together about activities that are offered through your community or your child's school. Talk to your child about limiting her activities and explain the different reasons for the limitations. Have her plan out a schedule and include homework time, practice time, family time, and downtime. Encourage her to choose activities that she really enjoys and let her know that she can try something else later if she feels she wants to. For example, if your daughter wants to play on both the volleyball and basketball teams at school and they both fall in the same season, that level of activity may be too much and practices and games may conflict, causing even more stress. Have her choose one sport at first, with the chance to try another sport the next season if she's still interested.

 ALERT!

Families with more than one child will have to be especially careful not to let one child dominate all of the time set aside for extracurricular activities, especially when one child seems to have more interests than another. Try to keep it even and fair as much as possible.

Having No Interests

Shy or withdrawn children often seem as if they have no interests. If this is your child, never fear. There are activities out there that will pique his interests. You just have to help your child find them.

You can start by talking to other parents about the activities their children enjoy. Ask your child if he would be more interested in pursuing an activity that a friend is already involved in. Call your community's information center about the activities they offer. Broaden your scope of activities. For instance, call art centers to see what classes they offer children. Try youth groups or Scouts that do different types of activities together. If you continue to encourage your child and give him the time and resources, he will find his interests.

 FACT

It is important that your child has some type of physical activity or she runs the risk of becoming overweight. Research has shown that the number of overweight kids in the United States is approaching 20 percent. A new study reveals that one in four obese children have early signs of type 2 diabetes—a type that was seen only in adults until recently.

Keep Your Child Involved

When your child wants to quit an extracurricular activity, step back and ask why. Then really listen to his answer. It may be that a teachable moment is in the making; maybe he had a spat with one of his teammates, in which case, quitting wouldn't be the answer. Or maybe he isn't up to practicing his piano lessons this week. But once he finishes practicing and accomplishes what he set out to do, he seems happier.

Perseverance is learned. In order for a child to learn it, though, there needs to be a time when he does not feel like doing something. But then he goes and does it anyway. A simple way to see if you should allow your child to stop doing an activity is to gauge his reaction to the activity while he's doing it, not just before he leaves for practice or a meeting. Many children have a hard time going from one thing to the next. They sometimes need a little push to get going but then have a wonderful time when they get there.

If your child does not enjoy an activity once he has become involved, it's okay to allow him to take a break from that activity. You should offer the option to pick up the activity again at a later date. It could be that your child was not ready for the experience and will grow into it eventually.

Make sure that your child is involved in some sort of extracurricular activity. Children need more than academics. They need the sense of accomplishment that extracurricular activities bring. If your child takes a break from the one activity he has, quickly replace it with another. You may have to dig around to find something that suits his interests, but it will be well worth the effort.

The Danger of Overextension

There is a fine line between cultivating your child's interest or talent and overextending her time to a point where she becomes stressed and unwilling to do anything. If you find yourself signing your child up for more than one activity at a time, stop and ask yourself why. Is it merely that more activities are being offered at the time, like in the beginning of the school year, or is it because you're trying too hard to give your child a head start on things she may be interested in later in life? Is she asking to be a part of everything, or are these separate activities that she can enjoy without stress? Whatever the reason, proceed with caution. Know that overextending your child in extracurricular activities will zap her energy and take away all of the fun. Not to mention taking you to the brink of insanity.

You may find yourself asking, "How many activities should my child be involved in?" This is a good question to ask yourself often, because your child may be involved in more activities at certain times of the year. If doing the activity is simple and fun for you and your child, then by all means do it. If adding another activity keeps things simple and fun, then allow your child to do that too. But as soon as the activities start to stress you or your child, you may need to take a look at which ones are not necessary and cut them.

Parents of more than one child find it all too easy to become overextended as a family. Along with your child's activities, you have responsibilities such as work, cleaning, laundry, and so on. When you're running in one direction and then another, trying to get child number one to soccer and child number two to ballet, fitting in the normal everyday household tasks can seem overwhelming. Here are a few tips to keep yourself from letting your family's schedule overwhelm you:

- Do mundane chores on a schedule and do them as quickly as possible. For example, make your bed as you get out of it.
- Every evening, make a to-do list for the next day.
- Before you go to bed, get your clothes ready for the next day.
- Use your family calendar to schedule all family appointments.
- Ten minutes before bedtime, have everyone in the family do a ten-minute pickup of the family living areas.
- Plan out your meals—breakfast, lunch, and dinner—for a full week, and then make your shopping list.
- Split your weekly cleaning to one or two jobs a day. Enlist the help of your family members.
- Keep a cleaning calendar. When you list out even the simplest chores, you take away the stress of having to remember what you have to do next.
- Do just one thing at a time. Once it's done, move on to the next item on your list.
- Schedule in a day off. Once a week order dinner in and let the household chores wait. (This only works if you schedule a certain day every week, not if you give up one day.)

Downtime Hobbies

A downtime hobby is something your child can do quietly at home. These include reading, collecting, making a scrapbook and writing in a journal, building models, doing crafts, and any number of other things. These hobbies are often done alone, but sometimes they are shared with family or friends. They are wonderful stress reducers and offer fun on rainy days. Find an activity that your child likes to do by starting him on one or two ideas, and then following through by providing the resources he needs. These also make for great gift ideas from relatives when you are having a hard time deciding what else your child could use.

Reading

Reading for pleasure is a great hobby. Often children are encouraged to read more, and enjoy it more, when they are given the opportunity to find books that pique their interests on a regular basis. Trips to the library and local bookstores at least once a month may persuade your child to pick up this downtime hobby if she isn't already an avid reader.

If your child does read often, point her to collections of books. Nancy Drew and the Hardy Boys are still doing a great job of capturing children's hearts today, and Harry Potter is a very popular series. When your child uses a book series for some downtime, she escapes into the wonderful comfort zone of a familiar character. Stress ebbs away. Be sure to get a list of all of the books in each series and keep it up-to-date by checking off which books your child has read.

Keeping Collections

Collecting is a great hobby because it can be unique for each child. When a child chooses something to collect, it makes a statement about what he likes, which helps define who he is. The possibilities for different collections are endless. It can be as simple as stamp collecting, or more involved like making ships in a bottle.

Collecting teaches children about sorting, organizing, keeping records, and labeling—all while becoming knowledgeable in a specific area of interest. Children learn about history, science, art, and more about themselves as they enjoy some stress-free downtime.

There is no limit as to what your child can collect. Think of your child's interests and put it into themes. Sports fans will like baseball or other sports cards. But that can even be expanded to memorabilia; a postage stamp of a sports player can start an interest in stamp collecting.

One word of caution; create a budget for your child's collecting and stick to it. This is a great way to teach your child the value of a dollar; some collectibles can become expensive. Do not, however, emphasize the monetary value of your child's collection. It should be done solely for his enjoyment, and not because he expects it to be worth money someday.

Arts and Crafts

While young children enjoy finger painting, the activity tends to lose its luster as your children grow older, which is a shame. There are a multitude of interesting arts and crafts that your child can choose from and would most definitely enjoy. From model building to jewelry making, there is something for everyone. Start by looking for ideas at your local library. You may even want to try your hand at something with your child. These can be a wonderful one-on-one or family activity.

Making a Scrapbook and Keeping a Journal

Older children love to play with pictures of themselves and snapshots of vacations, and then write about things that have happened. When you introduce kids to making scrapbooks and journals, you will be teaching them to take some time out to reflect. Then they will be able to keep these memories forever.

Teenage girls especially like to journal. If you feel this may be a good downtime hobby for your teenager, start by giving her a book and a nice pen—and then the right to write in it without fear that you will read it. Part of what makes a private journal rewarding is the privacy aspect.

Summertime Activities

Summertime is often downtime for extracurricular activities, since many are tied to school sports and clubs. This is also the time that families tend to take vacations and spend time together. But, it also leaves lag time for kids who are used to being busy. They may become bored and restless or lazy and hard to get motivated. Making a plan for the summer that includes your child's interests will help your child not become a couch potato.

Make a Plan

The first thing you want to do about summer vacations is plan out who is going to be doing what, and when they are going to do it. When you plan out your child's three months of summer vacation, you avoid the stress of not having something for your child to do. You'll avoid the "I'm bored" comments, and you will find that they will be more prepared to return to the hustle and bustle of the school year when it begins again. This is not to say that you have to plan out every minute of every day, or that your child needs to have something special to do at all times. A summertime plan is merely an organizational tool that will help you set expectations and reduce stress on you and your family.

 ESSENTIAL

Your child should have a say in what the summer plans are. Spend some time planning together as a family. Older children can help by trying their hand at putting together a budget or finding directions to a vacation spot on the Internet.

Start by planning your family vacations. Make family time come first when planning out the summer. Consider adding some different day trips or weekend jaunts to the calendar. Next plan your child's daily schedule. If both parents work, this will need to be done as soon as possible as children's centers and day-care camps fill quickly. If your child will be at home, create a daily plan that involves reading, daily chores, fun with friends, and downtime. If you schedule a weekly trip to the library, finding things to read will not be a problem for your child. While he should be responsible for completing daily chores throughout the year, you should be able to add one or two more small chores to his summertime schedule. This is a wonderful time to add a small responsibility because your child has the time to complete it. Children also need to keep in contact with their friends over the summer. If it is not feasible to plan play dates or activities with friends, encourage them to write letters or e-mail. Finally do not forget to schedule some downtime. Children can get overtaxed in the summer just as they can during the school year. Here are a few tips:

- Keep bedtimes early and on a regular basis. Just because your child no longer has to get up for school doesn't mean that she doesn't need her sleep. Later bedtimes with no consistency make for cranky morning children.
- Do not allow friend hopping. When your child gets together with one friend, comes home, and immediately goes out with another friend, that's friend hopping. Encourage your child to take a break between seeing friends and spend some time at home base.
- Remind him of his household and family commitments, if need be.
- Do not schedule more than one special activity in one day. Avoid placing things like basketball camp and swimming lessons in the same week.
- Try to make daily activities on a routine schedule. Eat lunch or go swimming at the same time every day so children know what to expect.

Benefits of Summer Camps

Day and overnight summer camps offer many benefits to children. Your child will grow at camp. She will become more independent and be more able to rely on her own resources. She will broaden her social skills and learn how to get along with many different types of people. This doesn't happen as often in the school arena as friends tend to form cliques.

Summer camps also teach new skills. Whether it's a sports camp or a nature camp, your child will learn many new things. A camp director's main goal is to have the children in the camp learn new and exciting things. This is how they ensure repeat business. They also keep kids very busy with activities; that is how they get your child to sleep soundly at night!

Teamwork and how to be responsible are also taught at day or overnight camps. Children learn to trust others and fulfill a need to work together through camp activities. Some camps even have specific trust-building activities such as a ropes course.

 **FACT**

Summer camps employ more than 1,200,000 adults as counselors, program/activity leaders, program directors/supervisors, and in support service roles such as maintenance, administration, food service, and health care. More than 12,000 day and resident camps of varying types, lengths, and sponsorships flourish in all parts of the United States.

Children as young as seven years old can enjoy the benefits of overnight summer camping, as long as they are properly prepared for the experience. Careful consideration needs to be taken when children go to an overnight camp this young. They should have previously experienced some type of day camp and the duration of the camp should not be any longer than a week. As your child gets older, the duration of his stay at camp can lengthen.

How to Choose a Summer Camp

One consideration when choosing a summer camp for your child is the cost. Summer camps can cost as little as $20 a day to as much as $200 a day. Private camps tend to be more costly, but they offer more in the area of special interests, such as sailing and extreme adventures. Nonprofit camps can be as good as their private counterparts, so take a good look at both to see if you can save some money. Make sure you inquire about the refund policy. If your child becomes sick or is otherwise unable to attend camp, you want to be sure you're not still going to have to foot the bill for the duration of the camp.

If you're worried about safety, the American Camp Association offers accreditation to camps, and some 2,300 day and overnight camps in America have earned it. The association publishes a book yearly called the *Guide to ACA-Accredited Camps.* However, many camps simply don't seek accreditation because of the cost involved.

Here are a few questions to ask camp directors and representatives when choosing a day or overnight camp for your child:

- What is the camp director's background? What are the backgrounds of the other camp staff?
- How much training has the staff had? Have they received specialized training from this camp?
- What are the ages of the camp counselors? What is the counselor-child ratio during the day? What is the counselor-child ratio at night?
- How are behavioral and disciplinary problems handled? Are positive reinforcement, assertive role modeling, and a sense of fair play used?
- Is the staff screened? Does the camp do use criminal background checks?
- What supervision does the staff receive? How do they prevent child abuse?
- What are the camp's policies on parent-camper communication? Are letters screened? Are phone calls allowed?

Getting Your Child Ready for Summer Camp

Togetherness is the key to getting your child ready for camp. Deciding which camp should always start with your asking your child what activities he would be interested in and going from there. Planning when and where should also be done as a family. When your child feels a part of this decision-making process, he will feel more in control and be more excited about the prospect of attending camp.

 ALERT!

Trust your instincts! If you're not comfortable with the camp director's answers, don't send your child to that camp, even if it looks good on paper. If you feel uncomfortable or uneasy about something, it's safest just to find another option. There are plenty of camps available; there is no reason to settle for something you may regret later.

Packing for camp is often a big hassle for parents. Make two copies of the camp's packing list when it comes in the mail, because it normally comes long before camp begins. Place the original copy in a safe-keeping spot in the house. Use the other two copies for packing: One for you and one for your child. This will help you avoid running around looking for the list the night before camp. Give your child the opportunity to pack his things by placing everything he needs on his bed. You can then check things off your list as you add them to his bag.

Camp Troubles

The biggest problem children face at camp is homesickness. This is a totally normal emotion, and every child goes through it at one point or another, even experienced campers. Preparing your child for homesickness beforehand often helps. Give her a sense of confidence in her abilities and describe the fun she will find at camp. You can also write often, and you may even want to write a letter to mail off the day she leaves for camp. Also, recognize that your child isn't the only one going through separation anxiety—so are you.

Keep procedures on how to contact the director of the camp handy in case a family emergency should come up. Know the procedures for having to pick up your child should there be a need. Have the phone numbers where others can find them in case something were to happen to you.

Summer camp can be a fun and exciting way to help your child grow and increase her skills and confidence level. The friends she will make at camp will last a lifetime.

CHAPTER 18

Attributes of a Successful Child

S UCCESSFUL CHILDREN have common traits or characteristics. There are five key traits that once mastered will lead a child to a happy and successful life. They are high self-esteem and self-worth, a willingness to learn, the ability to love, good character, and resilience.

Five Key Attributes of Successful People

Although there are no set formulas that will work with all children, there are common traits and characteristics of successful people. By using parenting skills and tools, you can encourage your children to develop these traits. You can help your children build the attributes they need to have a happy and successful life.

The successful child values himself and his abilities. He knows that he is worth your attention and affection, simply because he is your child. He has confidence that he can do what he sets out to do, even if it's new to him. He has high self-esteem and self-worth. The child who is on the road to success also has a willingness to learn. In fact you may be hard-pressed to stop him from learning (not that you'd want to!), because he will feel a need to learn. He will seem to devour everything when it comes to his areas of interest. He is willing to test out new ideas, dig for the answers, and proudly display his accomplishments. This attribute will take the successful child far in his academic life and gain him respect from his teachers and fellow students.

A child who has the ability to love will be able to surround himself with people who love and support him throughout his life. He will be able to use empathy when dealing with other people. He will know the joy of loving and being loved. He is also flexible. He goes with the flow and does not allow changes to cause him stress. He adapts to his limits even when he doesn't agree with them. He is willing to try things out before deciding whether he likes them. He is willing to compromise.

The successful child has good moral character. He is able to put his best foot forward when it is called for. He has manners, displays sportsmanship, and knows how to be kind. He works hard for what he wants and does not use anyone else to get it. He is the child who shows strength and whom people count on and trust.

 **FACT**

Appearances are important. Outward appearance in children is often a reflection of inner feelings. Encourage your teen to practice good hygiene and walk and talk with self-confidence. Give her confidence in her abilities so she can look people in the eye proudly.

Unfortunately, the road to success has its bumps. The successful child uses resilience to circumvent or deal with the repercussions of life's tough lessons. He is the capable kid who when faced with a challenge begins to look for answers. Although some children seem to have this attribute naturally, it is most often taught to them by their parents or by the school of hard knocks.

Why These Attributes Lead to Success

To be successful in life you need to be happy with you as an individual. Having these attributes will take your child to that point.

Self-Esteem and Self-Worth

Above all else, your child needs to value herself as a person. If she doesn't see herself as valuable, nothing else matters. That is how important your child's self-worth is; it is her basis for existing. Self-esteem comes in a close second in the level of importance. How your child values her own abilities will determine if she is willing to use those abilities.

When your child knows she has value and abilities that are valuable, she will develop a can-do attitude. She will feel capable and worthy of being loved. She won't be afraid of making mistakes, because she understands that mistakes happen and anything worth doing is worth the risk of making a mistake.

 ESSENTIAL

In the early years you are the sole support, builder, and guard for your child's self-esteem. As your child gets older, he will begin to rely on peers and other adults to perform some of these jobs for him.

Willingness to Learn

Without a willingness to learn, life will be an everyday struggle for your child. Children who are unwilling to learn shut down. They do not have the same social skills as their peers and generally become outcasts.

A child who is willing to learn will never be stopped by any obstacle that comes her way. She will tackle obstacles as problems to be solved, not as roadblocks that make her turn back. She will be able to seek out answers to her problems and find them.

The Ability to Love

Successful children need to love and be loved. It is a basic human need. With a loving foundation in his life, the successful child will look at the outside world with hope. He will carry joy in his heart and will want to contribute to society.

Children who are successful in their ability to love surround themselves with people who are loving as well. When you foster the ability to love in your child, you are giving him a gift of always having a loving relationship in his life, and he will seek out people like himself.

Good Character

The successful child needs good character in order to gain trust from those around her. She will slowly build her character and gain trust from others by accepting responsibilities and following through. Developing her character gives her stamina and teaches her the value of hard work and perseverance.

The little things about a child's character are also important in the road to success. Manners are really not a forgotten concept and are very important for children to learn. Sportsmanship will teach her how to play fairly. Striving to help others will teach her to appreciate what she has.

Resilience

Every day your child will face at least one challenge, probably many more. He needs to be able to face that challenge and work it out in order to be successful. He needs to bounce back when things don't go his way.

Resilient children can face failure and try again. They have a higher tolerance for frustration, exhibit impulse control, and are able to delay gratification. Resilient children become proficient in problem-solving and decision-making because of these skills. The successful child needs flexibility so he can deal with other people effectively. He needs to learn the art of compromise. He needs to learn to go with the flow in order to fit in with society. For instance, say you need to get your son and daughter to their soccer games at the same time on Saturday morning and then pick them up at the same time that afternoon. You work out a compromise that you will drop one off early and pick up the other late. A flexible child would see this as being fair and accept that he will have to wait a little bit.

Using Parenting Skills and Tools

You will use many if not all of your parenting skills and tools to foster each one of these attributes in your child. You will be using them daily, every moment in fact, as your child is always learning and growing. You'll need to keep your tools and skills handy because your child will be setting the pace most of the time.

 FACT

Keep parenting information handy to use in moments of crisis. If you are ever unsure of what to do with your child, simply take a break to figure it out using the information you have on hand. There is no rule that says you can't take some time to make a decision.

Communication and Modeling

What you say and do go hand in hand. You can foster each of the attributes of a successful child by using these two parenting tools correctly. But you can also send mixed messages if you use them incorrectly.

Sending mixed messages often occurs when parents are trying to teach the love of reading. You tell your child that reading is fun and that she should enjoy it. She hears that reading is necessary in school. But how often does she see you reading? Do you let her see you reading just for fun? Or is when you read to her the only time she sees you reading for fun? Are you communicating and modeling the same message?

Take a good look at your daily actions and reactions to see if they match up with what you want to communicate to your child. If you are unsure, ask her. She'll tell you.

Decision-Making and Problem-Solving

Using problem-solving as a parenting tool always involves using your decision-making skills. Therefore, they come packaged together pretty much all of the time. You will foster flexibility, resilience, a willingness to learn, and good character when you use them.

There are forks in the road when you are developing attributes for success. A child who can assess the situation, make a decision, and problem-solve will learn the lesson of the attribute he is working on, even if he makes the wrong decision and doesn't solve the problem correctly. By always having your decision-making skills and problem-solving tools handy, you will be able to support your child when he is faced with a dilemma. You will be able to walk him through the process of making good decisions that will solve his problem.

 ALERT!

Children grow in the preteen years almost as fast as they do when they are infants. These times are marked with growing pains, and preteens can often seem tired. Don't mistake this for laziness.

Support, however, does not mean you can make the decisions for him. It is extremely hard to take a step back and allow your child to make his own decisions and it gets harder as he grows older. When your child becomes a preteen, you will need to start allowing him to make decisions that you normally make and are comfortable making. For instance, if you always had your child on a spring soccer team because you like playing and coaching soccer, your child may decide to try baseball instead. This is his decision and you need to allow him to follow through with it, even if it means no more soccer for you. You do, however, have the ultimate veto power. If in this example, your child no longer wants to play any sport because he is being a little lazy, you can, and should, push him into doing something to stay active and involved.

Emotional Intelligence and Morals and Values

Building a strong family structure with your morals and values will help your child develop good character and enhance her ability to love. A person of good character, someone who works hard and values friendship can become successful in so many different areas. By using her perseverance, reliability, and trustworthiness, she will be able to grow relationships with people who have the same qualities.

By using your emotional intelligence, you will be able to read where your child is coming from and where her feelings lie. You will be able to tune into what moral issues she is having and, therefore, help her with her dilemmas. By taking the time to do this, you will be teaching her to take time to consider how other people are feeling when she is dealing with them. She will be more willing to help another person because she understands him or her.

When the World Steps In

There will be other people—people outside your family—in your child's life who influence his behavior. Teachers, coaches, Scout leaders, and friends' parents are a few of the other people your child interacts with regularly. These people are capable of affecting your child's attributes positively or negatively, depending on the type of people they are. When the results are positive, and other adults model behaviors that you wish your child to learn and support the values you believe in, this can be a powerful support tool for you. But when your views aren't supported, it can create an uphill battle with your child.

For instance, some parents of teenagers want to be their child's friend and remain "cool" in their child's eyes. They may allow their child to have sleepover parties where alcohol is served. Their thoughts are that the teenagers will just do it anyway, so why not supervise it? You, being totally against this, will not let your teenager attend. You would be right to do so. But your teenager is going to have a problem with it, because many of his friends will be there having a good time. The only way to deal with this is to be honest, and then allow him to own his feelings. Tell him you are sorry he is upset, and you hope he'll feel better soon. Do not give in.

As your child gets older, you will see more and more aspects of the world outside of your family that can be detrimental to everything you've worked for with your child. Have you seen the most popular music videos lately? They do not have your child's best interests at heart. For that matter, do you watch the news? Your child does not need to be exposed to all of that negativity. Censor your television for everyone in the family. Incorporate it into your family rules or plan. Only allow certain channels and enforce a time limit of three to five hours a week. Use the ratings on music and video games to censor them. Don't trust the ratings, however; there may still be something you find offensive in the music or game. Spend some time with your child playing the music or the game to see if you truly approve.

The Power of Peer Groups

Often, when parents think of peers, they fail to see the power that they hold as a positive influence on their child. When your child hits the preteen years, her peers will become very important to her. This does not mean, however, that she will automatically be taken in by a peer group that will steer her the wrong way.

Yes, your child and her group of friends will want to follow all the current fads. But, peers will not affect your child's abilities. More often than not, children find peers with similar abilities and values, thereby strengthening their own. You can use the power of your child's peer group to foster successful attributes in your child.

You can use your child's peer group to help find teachable moments. Your child's peers will place her in situations in which she needs to make decisions. Whether it's about a time schedule or a squabble, use these times to teach your child decision-making skills. Decisions will be harder for your child to make when she is being influenced by others. Therefore, you can teach her to be flexible and compromise, or how to take a stand with respect to her friends' needs. Peers will also help your child make a stand against drugs or violence. There is safety in numbers—your child will feel safe when she is with a friend who will also say no to these things. Reinforce this teachable moment by praising your child and praising her choice of friends.

Peers can also give your child something to do. Did you know that children as young as eleven years old are capable of doing volunteer work for their church or community? Starting at this age, children love doing something meaningful. It boosts their self-esteem and self-confidence. The trick is for you, the parent, to step away from the picture and allow your child and her friends to own the job. While you should be involved in organizing the event, the more hands-off you are as a supervisor, the more the kids will enjoy it. Children this age love to own what they are doing. So set it up and let them. You'll get to see firsthand how well the power of peers works.

 **FACT**

Encourage your child not to belong to the popular crowd. Many times children who belong to this crowd become overly stressed. They become so involved with what others want from them that they never explore what genuine friendship is all about.

Time Will Tell

It takes nature eighteen years to produce an adult. So don't get discouraged when you are working on building your child's attributes and it seems as if it is taking forever for him to get a handle on it. He may also need to relearn some things as he grows and changes developmentally. There are a few areas in which time is all that is needed.

Time and Self-Confidence

Self-confidence is a funny thing. It is always being tested. Humans gain self-confidence with experience, so every time your child tries something new, his self-confidence is tested. He just needs the time to adjust and gain the experience. Colleges understand this. They tend to give first-semester freshmen a break on their workload by giving them general classes and not allowing them to load up on credits. They know that your child needs time to adjust to being away from home. They understand that your child's self-confidence just needs a little time.

Time and Discipline

Often parents get frustrated when their discipline method doesn't seem to be working. They set a limit and their child waltzes right by it, so they give a consequence. Their child pays her dues and then waltzes right by the limit again. The parents throw up their hands and say, "Well, that didn't work!" They flounder around, not knowing what to do next, or they up the consequence to an impossible height. What they have failed to remember is that sometimes children need more time to learn. Sometimes, they need to make the mistake more than once or twice . . . or ten times, for that matter. One key factor in discipline is consistency. The main ingredient in consistency is time.

CHAPTER 19

High Self-Esteem and Self-Worth

A CHILD WITH A HEALTHY SELF-ESTEEM has a can-do attitude. He feels capable, responsible for his actions, and worthy of love. He values himself and believes he has worth. He knows that he can make his life what he wants it to be. He is capable of success in life.

Two Important Qualities

Children need self-esteem and self-worth in order to be able to take charge of their own lives. This is not to say that they need to control, actually the opposite is true. A child with a healthy self-esteem and self-worth can be a follower or a leader, whichever the situation calls for. She is comfortable in both roles because she has a solid belief in herself and her abilities.

In order to understand why children need both self-esteem and self-worth, it is important to know the difference between these qualities. Self-worth is a belief that you have a reason to exist. Self-esteem springs off that base and builds confidence in your abilities.

Self-worth is a feeling of value. It is the belief that you are valuable simply because you are a human being. It gives credence to the fact that you deserve to be loved because you exist. People with no self-worth feel worthless all of the time. They believe they have nothing to contribute because they have no value to begin with. People with low self-worth give up on life.

ESSENTIAL

If your child has a problem with his self-worth, it is time to seek some professional help. While some parents steer clear of getting professional help at all costs because of a perceived stigma against therapy, the successful parent knows better. Getting help is a sign of a parent who recognizes what is best for his or her child.

Self-esteem is a belief in your abilities. Having self-esteem means knowing you have valuable abilities and are a capable human being. It is the pride you feel when you accomplish a task. It is your belief that you can accomplish what you set out to do.

You can have self-worth and have low self-esteem, but you cannot have low self-worth and a high self-esteem. You can value yourself as a human being and not believe in your capabilities, but you cannot not value yourself as a human being and have a healthy outlook on your abilities.

Trying New Things

A child with a healthy self-esteem isn't afraid of trying new things. He enjoys the adventure in life. He can visualize a desire and put it into action. He isn't afraid of mistakes because he knows that mistakes occur, but having the chance to do something he desires is worth the risk. If he fails, he will try again until he succeeds. This trial-and-error process will lead to an even healthier self-esteem.

For instance, a toddler will try to learn how to walk down a step, even though she already knows how to turn around and go down the stairs backward. Why does she do this? Generally, it's because she is trying something that she sees everyone else doing. The first time she will most likely fall and sustain a few bumps or bruises. After a couple of soothing words from Mom or Dad, she will go back and try that very same step again.

Making Good Choices

A child with a healthy self-esteem is capable of weighing his options and making good choices. He will take the time to weigh the consequences of his potential actions. He will take a sound look at the people around him and pick friends who add value to his life.

For example, a second-grader tends to say what he means and mean what he says. If he is given a choice between two friends to play with, he will choose one and tell the other exactly why he didn't choose him. He may say something like "You're too bossy." While children in this age group are low on tact, they are very good at protecting their self-esteem.

Accepting Blame

A child with a healthy self-esteem takes the blame when she makes a mistake. She will look back at the situation and try to find areas where she could have done something differently. She will learn something from her mistakes and try again, even if she knows she may make a mistake again.

An older teenager who has had a breakup with a girlfriend is able to look back and see what was wrong with the way he handled a particular situation or with the views he took toward the relationship. He will not blame the other person for the breakup but will take a look at where he could have done things differently. He will learn why his personality did not go well with the other person's personality. He will accept that and move on and eventually date someone different.

Goal Setting and Planning

Children are always striving toward a goal, whether they define it for you (or themselves) or not. When they are young, they tend to know what they want, will plan how to achieve their goals on their own, and keep you guessing as to how they accomplished their task. Take, for example, a toddler who spies a book lying on the bed of her older sibling. If you had the opportunity to watch her face, you could see the goal form: "I want that book." She toddles over to the bed, looks at her goal, and plans how to get it. Her foot goes up, she grabs the blanket and pulls. After a few tries ending with her padded bottom on the floor, she may accomplish the goal of getting the book off the bed.

This isn't to say that you shouldn't work on setting goals and planning them out with your children—quite the contrary. Life gets more difficult as people grow, and goals become much more complicated than trying to get up on a sibling's bed. It is a gradual process, and it takes self-esteem to keep setting new goals and trying to reach them.

 FACT

> When parents set unrealistic goals for their children, children will suffer in two ways. One, they will not be able to meet their goal; therefore, they will not feel a sense of accomplishment and will not boost their self-esteem. Two, they will lose their trust in their parents' ability to set goals for them.

Infants tend to learn how to achieve their goals as they go. Trial and error helps them along as they learn to roll over, crawl, and eventually walk. Toddlers often use trial and error, too. This is why we spend so much time chasing after two- to three-year-olds as they explore the world around them. But as they are learning to communicate more, they are capable of setting a goal. It is beneficial to this age to make each goal one step away. You can help your child by using an "if/then" statement, giving your child one thing to accomplish to reach a goal. For example, "If you want to go outside, then you need to put your shoes on."

When children reach school age, they are capable of doing more than one step, but you still need to plan each step. That never changes. Planning goals means breaking them down into simple tasks. If you always use simple tasks when planning their goals, your children will always be able to see the path to a goal.

Your Reinforcing Role

As a parent, you will help your child build her self-esteem by planning for instances when you can help boost her sense of worth and minimizing the occasions where it is likely to be torn down. This is your reinforcing role. You cannot build your child's self-esteem for her; she will need to do that. But you do influence her self-esteem. A person who goes through childhood without a parental figure reinforcing her self-esteem is still capable of building a healthy self-esteem; it's just a much harder task.

Be a Positive Role Model

Plan to be a positive role model. Share your daily accomplishments. Take responsibility for your actions. When you make a mistake, verbalize how you will fix it and avoid making the same mistake the next time, and then follow through. Be realistic about your abilities and do not be overly harsh on yourself. Try and try again when things don't come out the right way.

 ALERT!

Modeling positive behavior is as important to your child's self-esteem as shaking off your bad habits. Verbalize what you are doing as you are doing it. Saying "I'm trying to do better" is teaching your child to try, which is the first step to succeeding.

Praise Often and Well

Praise your child when he accomplishes something. Praise the judgment he used to accomplish this task. For example, if your child scores a goal in the soccer game, he did very well. But it would be better to praise all of the practice he did the week before that led to him being able to score the goal, rather than just praising the act of scoring. Then he will continue to practice and still feel good about it if at the next game he isn't given the opportunity to score a goal.

Be wary of praising just for the sake of praise. If you praise your child when she doesn't deserve it, she will know. Then when you praise her the next time, she won't believe you. If you embellish your praise, you may also run the risk of it backfiring. For instance, if you call your child a genius because she got an A on her math test, she may think, it's too hard to be a genius. Then she will strive not to get an A the next time, so she doesn't have to live up to the expectation of being a genius.

Affection Is a Must

Affection is a form of praise that children can never get too much of. Hugs and kisses are special and need to be given often. "I love you" needs to be said more than once a day in both words and actions. Smiles and laughter need to be part of your household, even when times are tough.

Build a Safe and Nurturing Environment

Living in a safe environment is essential to self-esteem. A child needs to feel safe and secure. He needs to know that his basic necessities will be met. A child who is abused physically or does not have his basic needs, such as food, will not be able to work on his self-esteem. He may even begin to lose value in himself as a human being, thereby lowering his self-worth.

Help Your Child Become Involved

There is a point in your child's life when you may begin to feel like a chauffeur rather than a parent. This is especially true when you have more than one child, but it can also happen with one. Children with a healthy self-esteem tend to enjoy becoming involved in many different activities. This helps boost their self-esteem even higher as they learn new things and accomplish new tasks.

If you can keep up with their schedules, it is beneficial in many ways to keep your child in as many activities that she can handle. An active child is one who doesn't have time for trouble, she has a strong pool of peers from which she can choose good friends, and she learns new things outside of the school structure. If you have a hard time keeping up with her busy schedule, try car-pooling with friends, getting her involved in afterschool activities when a bus is provided, or doing the activity with her. Scouting has positions for parents as well as their children. Community classes on art, first aid, or computers are fun to take with your child.

Gender Differences in Self-Esteem

For reasons not yet totally defined by the experts, boys and girls look at themselves differently. This self-image has a major effect on their self-esteem. It also explains why they act so differently when they reach adolescence.

Boys Internalize Accomplishments

Boys tend to internalize accomplishments and externalize faults. That is to say that when a young man does something right, he will feel that the reason it was done correctly was him, but if that task does not work out, he will find blame in something else rather than take the responsibility for it. In this way, boys protect their self-esteem and can have problems with an overly high self-esteem.

Girls Externalize Accomplishments

Girls, on the other hand, tend not to take pride in their accomplishments because they feel they were not responsible for the accomplishment. They will, however, place undue blame on themselves when anything they're involved with goes wrong. Girls are harder on themselves. They leave their self-esteem out in the open to be battered. They externalize accomplishments and internalize faults.

This can lead to a negative body image in their preteen years. They will compare themselves to others, often the models in the teen magazines they read. Girls need to be encouraged to set realistic expectations. They need to be reminded that they *have* earned their accomplishments. You will need to be there to tell them. Do so often.

Problems to Look Out For

Most children will face issues related to low self-esteem at some point. It is simply a normal part of growing up. It can be scary to face a challenge that is new or that does not have an obvious or quick solution.

 FACT

Self-image is how you see yourself in relation to others. It's what you think you look like physically, how you feel your personality comes across, and what you think others think of you.

An example of this is when children enter kindergarten. They will encounter children of all different backgrounds with different levels of knowledge. Some children may already know much of what is taught in kindergarten, while others haven't been exposed to the kind of learning involved. Kindergarten teachers will help children at all levels reach the level they need to move on to first grade. Therefore, some of the children will be reviewing what they already know and some will be learning new things. But the children notice the difference and immediately label who is smart in the class and who isn't. This may be the first time your child has been confronted with a peer who seems to do "better" than he does at something. And that can be hard on his self-esteem at first. You have to be ready when this happens and help guide him lovingly through it, so these issues don't become problems.

There are always challenging times in life. Your child's self-esteem will bounce up and down as she realizes and faces these challenges. There is never one correct way to get around challenges or prepare for them. You have to deal with situations as they arise. Remain supportive and encouraging. Help your child with the specifics. For instance, if it is a math class that your son is having a hard time with, tell him all about the time you had a hard time with math, and hire a tutor to help. Let him know that he's not alone in having challenges to face.

Puberty is probably the most challenging time for children and their parents. Again, there is no correct way to prepare for it because all children's situations entering puberty are different. Some start early; others start late. Whatever the case with your child, you will need to help her deal with the challenge of her changing body as it happens. Open communication and encouragement from you at this time will help her face new challenges with her self-esteem intact.

 ESSENTIAL

> The language of self-esteem says things like "I don't understand this" instead of "I'm an idiot." How you talk to and about yourself sets the mood for how you act.

Activities That Foster High Self-Esteem

Most activities that foster high self-esteem and self-worth involve cooperation rather than competition. They offer an opportunity for the child's unique abilities to stand out. They reinforce, nurture, and strive to help the child with their talents. They continue to build in complexity as the child continues to grow.

Activities for Babies and Toddlers

Babies and toddlers are doers. Anything that gets their attention and encourages them to do something is a great activity for boosting their self-esteem. Lively music and colorful shapes or books will promote action that you can praise. Give him your loving attention and maintain a positive outlook. Your baby doesn't really need a lot more to begin developing a healthy self-esteem.

Activities for School-Age Children

One challenge school-age children face is being without their parents for long periods. Kids in this age group need praise when they do something right. The problem lies in the fact that there are often twenty-five to thirty of them in a class and one teacher cannot be expected to praise each child for everything he or she does correctly. One activity that you can do with your child that will help her learn how to congratulate herself is giving "palm kisses." Before your child leaves for school, kiss her palm, and then close her hand. Tell her that the kiss is for her to use later, when she does something good. When she comes home from school ask her what she used the kiss for.

You can also try some of these simple ways to boost children's self-esteem around home:

- Display good schoolwork on the refrigerator.
- Use a sticker calendar for marking down when they brushed their teeth or made their bed.
- Thank them when they help you.
- Spend time listening to them talk about their day.
- Put love notes in their school lunches.
- Play a game with them that they are as capable of winning as you are.
- Accept them when they aren't perfect and tell them you are happy they have done their best.

Remind your school-age child that there are things about him that he cannot change. He will not be able to change anything about the shape of his nose or the color of his skin. These are the things that make each person unique. They make him special and different—remind him of this if he seems concerned.

Activities for Teens

Teach teenagers how to use self-talk in a positive way. When teens talk to themselves encouragingly, they step over the obstacles that life or their peers may put in their way. The reason self-talk works is very simple. Thoughts precede how you feel, your moods. If you think you are feeling unhappy, you will act unhappy. If you think and tell yourself you are not capable, you are that much further away from being capable.

Practicing affirmations can help your teenager get in the habit of positive self-talk. Some affirmations to have them try include the following:

- "I am capable."
- "I am friendly."
- "I have a beautiful smile."
- "I have positive opinions."
- "I am an honest person."
- "I am good at _____ (*fill in the blank*)."

Building a healthy self-esteem in your child and helping her maintain it as she grows up is essential to her success. She will be much better equipped to handle challenges and take on new ambitions when she believes in herself.

CHAPTER 20

The Willingness to Learn

Y OUR CHILD'S BRAIN is wired to learn. She is more than willing to take in anything and everything and process that information from the time she is born. Turning this instinct into an ongoing love of learning is what will help her be successful.

Learning Is the Key to the Future

Learning brings understanding of life's situations when people are faced with problems and need solutions. When children have a willingness to learn, they open doors for themselves. Children who enjoy learning have greater self-confidence. They know they can find answers to their questions. When parents encourage the love of learning, they add to their child's self-confidence, bringing them even closer to success.

Home Environment That Encourages Learning

A secure home life where your child feels the love you have for him is the foundation for learning. Good nutrition, plenty of sleep, and regular exercise are all needed to promote a home environment that encourages learning. Establish routines and good habits such as nightly reading, to ensure nonstressful learning experiences. Enrich your home with activities that promote learning. Make a special place for homework to be done, in a calm and quiet atmosphere.

Children who have to waste time searching for their shoes or study notes among a lot of clutter do not enjoy an environment that encourages learning. Work on developing good habits in all areas of a child's life in order to provide a stable environment.

Organization and Study Skills

Good study skills are a must. In order for your child to develop them, she first needs to become organized. Planners are a must for older, school-age children, and younger children can benefit by getting into the habit of using them also. By eliminating the stress of having to remember what work needs to be done, your child will be able to dig into the work itself. Teach her how to organize by helping her put her papers away daily. When she has finished with a paper, verbalize where it goes. Children in middle school may need to be reminded here and there also; they are likely to become disorganized at this age. Hang a calendar in your child's room for her to write important dates on, such as the dates of upcoming tests, field trips, days off, and so on.

 **FACT**

According to research done by Jupiter Communications, in 2002, 44 million children ages two to twelve had access to and used the Internet. That is 47 percent of all kids in that age group. This was up from 36 percent in 2001 and 26 percent in 2000.

While you do not have to turn your home into a library, it is important to have certain reference material and school supplies handy. A dictionary and calculator are a must—just ask any parent who has had to check their fourth-grader's long division problems.

A computer with Internet access is an excellent tool to have at home. There is nothing like having the Library of Congress at your fingertips when your child has a history paper due. The small things are just as important. Pens, pencils, pencil sharpener, colored pencils, and paper are all needed items. Stock up during the back-to-school sales and help your child be prepared at home as well as at school.

Tackling Homework

Your child has homework. No matter how much he tells you differently, he has it. You need to set up a homework routine in your daily schedule. Your child needs a quiet time and place to do homework daily. That is every school day, even if he has study halls at school. Yes, it is stressful with everything else that needs to get done in the evening, but it is imperative to your child's academic success.

To reduce the stress, set up the routine. Once everyone is used to following it, the stress will subside. You may try to have homework time right after school or dinner. Spend a few minutes in the beginning of his homework time praising any good things that happened that day, and encourage him to do better in any areas he fell short. Try not to criticize poor grades but problem-solve for the next time. What does your child think went wrong? What could he do differently the next time? Be encouraging and supportive about the grades, and be strong and persistent about the routine. You'll be teaching him how to work hard toward a goal, which leads to reaching that goal successfully.

 ESSENTIAL

By sixth grade, your child will need to spend an hour nightly going over her schoolwork and doing her homework. When a child gets into high school and has study halls, she should still have a set time to do some work at home.

Maximizing Academic Achievement

Every parent wants to help his or her child in the classroom. The question often is how? Many times, you may feel that you are on the outside looking in. Parents often are. This feeling is often cited by parents as the reason for homeschooling their children. It's understandable. You were the number-one source of information for your child until they reached school age. Then, all of a sudden, other sources of authority become very prominent in your child's life.

In order to maximize your child's academic achievement, you will need to accept your child's school system for what it is—a place for him to learn. You will need to set realistic expectations about your child's teacher. You will need to accept the fact that other people now have some control over what your child is learning. Once you've accepted that, it is easier to see your role in your child's academic future. It is your job to oversee, to prepare your child every day, and to encourage and support.

 **FACT**

According to the U.S. Department of Health and Human Services, involvement by fathers in children's schooling, such as volunteering at school and attending school meetings, parent-teacher conferences, and class events, is associated with higher grades, greater school enjoyment, and lower chances of suspension or expulsion from school.

Your Role as an Overseer

As an overseer, you will manage your child's education. You will decide if you should send your child to public or private school, or perhaps you will decide that homeschooling is the answer for your family. You will talk to your child about her school day. You will attend parents' nights and communicate with your child's teachers as often as possible. When she gets older, you will help her choose classes that will guide her toward her goals in life. You will do your best to keep on top of the situation at school without nitpicking her teachers (an all-too-common trap that parents can fall into).

Your Preparatory Role

It can be easy to miss things in the morning rush to get your kids ready for school. Too many families do not take the time in their busy morning schedule to sit down and enjoy a meal before they start their day. They've gotten into the habit of getting up at the last minute and running around the house in the morning trying to get everything done in order to get out the door. Therefore, children feel rushed and stressed before they even get to school. If this sounds like your family, try this routine:

In the evening:

- Choose what outfits everyone will wear the next day.
- Prepare lunches or lunch money.
- Sign all papers that need to be signed.
- Have your child pack his backpack and place it by the door, include sneakers for gym, band instrument, etc.
- Write a to-do list of errands you need to do the next day.

In the morning:

- Get up one-half hour earlier than your child.
- Get dressed and ready.
- Wake your child with a smile.
- Have breakfast together.

If you force yourself to do this routine for thirty days, it will become a habit. Everyone will start his or her day less stressed and will enjoy this time together. The benefits far outweigh anything the extra thirty minutes in bed would get you.

Your Encouraging and Supporting Role

It's important for you to watch your attitude when dealing with your child and her academics. You need to allow your child to own her education. You will need to allow her to make her own mistakes, but be there when she asks for help. That doesn't mean letting her do whatever she wants whenever she wants. It means that together you set up the plan and then you let her follow it. For example, have a discussion about when she would like to complete her homework every evening. With the time set, a quiet place, and materials available, she should be able to follow through with getting her homework done. You should not feel the need to sit with her and make sure each question is done correctly. That is micromanaging the situation and will lead her to have bad feelings about her homework.

Teacher and School Problems

There are times when your child may not click with a teacher. As a parent you need to accept this situation as okay and still doable for your child. If you think about how many years your child will be in school and how many teachers he will have, you will realize that they will not love each and every one. Even the ones they do love will cause them grief once in a while.

When, however, you have a major problem with a school or teacher, you will need to communicate your dissatisfaction to them. For instance, suppose a teacher wrongly accused your child of cheating. You can step in. Do so by writing a letter and dropping it off at the school. Copy the immediate supervisor, principal, or school administrator. Start off with, "It is my understanding that . . ." Then name the incident. Do not rant. Do not rave. Every story has two sides and you will need to hear both. If the incident did occur, request a meeting with the teacher and the principal. In the meeting, remain calm and ask how they will go about fixing this problem. Offer your suggestions. If you handle a problem in this fashion, you will look like a team player, instead of an opponent.

If your problem is with the school itself, you will need to document the problem and forward it to the principal and school board. If you feel alone in this situation, start talking to other parents and see where their feelings lie. You may find you have more backing than you think. Petitions, letters in the local newspaper, and school board meeting attendance tends to do wonders when dealing with issues such as hot lunches constantly being served cold.

You do have the right, and responsibility, to check on the school and voice your opinion as a parent. Before you do, though, check that your expectations aren't too high. Be a team player and listen to all sides. Weigh the pros and cons to speaking up or finding an alternative way to fixing the problem.

Communication Between Parent and Child

Talk to your child daily about school. If she continually brings up problems such as a child next to her constantly talking and disturbing her while she is doing her work or other children being mean at recess, encourage her to handle the problem on her own. Help her come up with ways to solve the problem. Encourage conflict resolution by going through the suggested solutions and weighing the pros and cons. Follow through by asking her how it went the next day. If the problem wasn't solved, rewind and repeat. These things take time.

If you find your child only gives short answers to questions about his day at school, it may be because he does not feel you really want to know or that you're only concerned with how he is doing scholastically instead of how he is feeling about his school life. And make no mistake about that. Your child will be spending over 16,000 hours in school for his first thirteen years. That's over 600 full twenty-four-hour days. School is not just something he does; it's very much a part of his life, complete with social aspects and stress. So ask specific questions about his school life to show you are interested in his day, not just what grades he is making.

Your child knows that you want him to do well in school. When you state expectations for grades, you do not need to pound in that point. Instead, state expectations on things you can control at home. For instance, instead of expecting certain grades, expect that he will study for one hour at a time you set together and a place you set together. Instead of expecting a B in math, expect him to use at least twenty minutes of his study time on math. In this way, you set him up to succeed. You've set up small steps for him that are doable. By doing them, he will keep on top of his schoolwork and be able to achieve his goals.

ALERT!

Talking to your child about her day is as important as feeding her dinner. Listen to what her day was like and enjoy the conversation. If she doesn't seem up to talking, try adding dessert to the dinner menu that evening. Children love to talk over ice cream.

Communication Between Parent and Teacher

In the beginning of the school year, write your child's teachers a note introducing yourself. Let them know you are open to talking with them at any time. Stress that although you feel there won't be any problems, should they arise you would like to be informed. When your child is in elementary school, have him take the notes in to his teacher. When your child enters middle school, it's time to mail them or drop them off yourself. For an older child you may also ask the teacher not to mention the note to your child in front of his peers, as that is embarrassing. This is a great way to break the ice between parent and teacher and ensures a decent conversation on the first parents' night.

Notes are a great way to communicate with your child's teacher when she is young. As your child gets older, however, phone calls are necessary to handle small problems that can occur, such as your child being absent on the day of a test. You can also talk to the guidance counselor if the teacher is unavailable.

When attending a parents' night, be yourself. Let the teacher know that you are a team player and very interested in your child's academics. Ask him if there will be a time in the school year when he could use your help. Find out how he prefers you to contact him with a concern.

Learning Outside the Box

An experience that has value to your child will teach him something. That experience does not have to be taught in a classroom. Learning is ongoing. It does not stop when your child walks out of school. She may learn more about physics by pitching a baseball then she would in science class. That is human nature. Experiences with value to her will teach her more than regurgitating information. Parents can supplement this type of learning by pointing out how the experience connects with the information. For instance, you can explain to your daughter that where she releases the baseball changes the trajectory of the pitch. Or, you may see something on television that talks about local history, giving you an opening to teach your child a little more about her hometown. Whatever it is, never miss an opportunity to teach your child outside the box.

Problems to Look Out For

Many children have trouble in school. Some have trouble learning to read or write. Others have a hard time remembering new information. Still others may have trouble behaving. Children can have all sorts of problems. While these problems are difficult to handle at the time, it does not mean your child will be unsuccessful. On the contrary, often children who have to work harder in school become very successful. Schools are equipped to handle these problems and help your child succeed.

It's important to find out why a child is not doing well in school. The child may have a disability. By law, schools must provide special help to eligible children with disabilities. This help is called special education and related services.

You may ask the school to evaluate your child, or the school may ask you for permission to do an evaluation. If the school thinks your child may have a disability and may need special education and related services, they must evaluate your child before providing your child with these services. This evaluation is done at no cost to you. The evaluation will reveal if your child has a disability and what kind of special help your child needs in school.

 **FACT**

One out of every five people in the United States has a learning disability. Almost 3 million children (ages six through twenty-one) have some form of learning disability and receive special education in school. In fact, over half of all children who receive special education have a learning disability.

There are four steps to the evaluation, which is typically done by a group of school administrators and teachers, and must always include you as well. The first step is to examine what is already known about your child. Does the group need more? If so, the school must collect it. The second step is collecting additional information (with your permission), which may be done in a number of ways, such as diagnostic tests. Third, the school will decide your child's eligibility for special education and related services. Based on the evaluation results, the group of school professionals and you, the parents, decide. Fourth, if your child is eligible, you and the school will develop an educational program to meet your child's needs.

Activities That Foster Willingness to Learn

You as the parent engage in many of the activities that foster willingness to learn. Continue to encourage and support your child with her schoolwork. Point out and enjoy life experiences with your child. Most of all: Read! Modeling this good habit will not only benefit your child, but you will enjoy it.

Activities for Babies and Toddlers

Reading is the number-one activity for babies and toddlers. They can never have enough access to books. They love to hear your voice and even though they may not understand the stories, they do begin to have favorite books.

Music and children's music videos also stimulate early learning. Allow your child to dance around as she watches, and dance around with her. One of the joys of parenting is being able to act young again, so don't miss this opportunity.

Activities for School-Age Children

Reading is still the number-one activity for children as they grow. When children reach school age, they will begin to start reading on their own, although enjoying a book together is even more fun because they can follow the story and begin discussing it. Get your child a library card and start a routine of going to the library weekly. Get a list of recommended books from teachers or other parents. Use it to give out ideas for Christmas or birthday presents. Children this age love going to a bookstore with a gift certificate. (As an added bonus, this activity teaches them about managing money.)

Hands-on is the key phrase for this age group. They are getting enough memorization practice in the classroom. Promote more right-brain learning by offering your child craft kits, clay, paint, models, and so on.

ESSENTIAL

School-age children feel a sense of accomplishment every time they bring a library book home, read it, and return it on time. Have a special place in your home to store library books so you won't be on a scavenger hunt every time library day rolls around.

Activities for Teens

Reading will remain the number-one activity that encourages learning throughout your child's lifetime. It will add dimension to his personality, as he becomes an individual. It will be his number-one source of information, whether he reads books, magazines, newspapers, information on the Internet, and so on. Encourage him to read for enjoyment daily, even if it's just the comics in the newspaper. A weekly library routine is still a great idea, but you can also offer to take one of his friends with you each week.

Experiences at this age are a must to promote learning. Encourage your child to become part of an active youth organization. Allow them to be on the go-go-go; they have the energy. The more involved they are in learning experiences, the less time they have for the troubling world to step in.

CHAPTER 21

The Ability to Love

To LOVE AND BE LOVED is one of humankind's greatest abilities. A child who knows that she is loved has the strongest foundation for her self-esteem and self-confidence. With that foundation, she is capable of passing on her love successfully.

Knowing How to Love

Children need to feel loved in order to love back. When children can love and show affection, they receive love back. They are able to form deep relationships that enhance their self-esteem and self-confidence. There is only one way to give your child the ability to love and that is to love him fully. You need to love him with every fiber of your being. The love you feel for your child is so vast and has such depth that it is simply inexplicable.

The problem you face when you love someone this much is the fact that you need to show your child your love in different ways. Some are the traditional ways that you show everyone affection. But others are very different, and that is what can make them very hard to do.

Communicating Your Love

As you know children learn through example, or modeling, so it is important that you express your love for your child often. A simple "I love you" goes far when she is off to school or out with a friend. You can also express your love through touch by caressing her, patting her on the back, or giving her a hug. You can do this all through her childhood and into her adulthood. It is a right you earn as a parent. Unfortunately, many parents forget that they can enjoy this right.

Observe your child and brag about her to other people, especially when she is in earshot. Children love to hear when they are doing well, and it is an added bonus if she overhears it. It will tell her that you love her enough to pay attention to what she does.

Express your love through holding fast to the limits you have placed on your child. It takes a lot of love to do this. You as her parent must be her security at times, and when you hold fast to the limits, you give her the security and love she needs.

When your child progresses slowly toward a goal, cheer her on. Remember praise is accepted when it is warranted, so verbalize exactly what you are praising when you are praising it. Let her know that you are confident that she can make it, that she can accomplish what she has set out to do.

 ALERT!

> You will sometimes need to ask your child's permission to get a hug. It is impolite to hug someone who does not want to be hugged. If you are getting those vibes from your child, simply ask first.

Be there for her. If she is on the soccer team, go to the practices as well as the games. Offer to help the coach or do other tasks for the team. Cheer loudly and help her learn the lessons of sportsmanship. Be active in what she does in school. Go to school parents' nights and talk about what you heard. Enjoy conversations with her and give her your undivided attention. Set up some one-on-one time with her.

Kindness and Courtesies

When your child has the ability to love, he is capable of kindness to family, friends, and strangers. He can show empathy. He learns how to walk in another's shoes before making a judgment. He offers to help people when they are in need. These actions help increase his self-esteem, and he will benefit by having strong personal relationships with friends. He will be respected by others and enjoy having people around him who are just as kind as he is, because people tend to surround themselves with other people who are like them.

Walking a Mile in Another's Shoes

Learning to walk a mile in another's shoes is a hard lesson to learn. It means you have to step away from your own feelings on a particular matter and literally feel what another is feeling. A child who has a healthy emotional intelligence is capable of learning how to do this. It is critical that your child learn how to do this so she can learn how to show kindness and help other people out.

Children are capable of seeing things from another's point of view when they reach school age. You can promote this when your child talks to you about her day in school. Ask her how she thinks another person felt or how she would feel if the same thing happened to her. When you show your child how to walk in another's shoes, you are beginning to teach her how to help other people, which is a form of affection. When you help someone, you are being kind because the other person is worth it, whether he is a friend or not.

Other Ways to Learn Helping

One way to model helping is to help together. Sign up to help with a community project or a school or church function. You will enjoy some time together as a family, or you can make this a one-on-one time event.

Teach your child how to take care of others. You can start this just as soon as he starts showing affection. Toddlers know how to give hugs when someone needs it, so ask for a hug when you are in need. Babysitting is a great way for preteens to learn how to take care of another person.

Unequal Treatment of Siblings

When you treat your children unequally, you will promote rivalry that isn't the normal sibling rivalry. Many parents don't even realize that they may treat their children differently. Many mothers dote on their sons as fathers dote on their daughters; then in turn they are harder on their same-sex children. Babies get much more attention than older children, out of necessity. But you will need to give your older child a little extra attention when there is a baby in the house. If you keep these circumstances in mind and do your best to balance out your attention, you will be blessed with nothing more than your typical normal sibling rivalry.

Sibling rivalry is a good thing! Yes, it's a frustrating, pull-your-hair-out, make-you-want-to-scream thing, but it's still a good thing. Children learn sympathy, respect for others, how to deal with other personalities, how to measure their worth, and the obvious, how to argue respectfully.

Direct mediation is not always required. Actually, if you step into an argument between siblings, it's likely to make it worse. It reinforces fighting as a way to get your attention. Of course, if your children are screaming at the top of their lungs, or hurting each other, looking the other way isn't going to do much good either, so you need to set the rules beforehand. The most important rule to set is on physical violence. Make it clear to your children that physical violence is not allowed. Children who wouldn't normally even think of hitting another person are usually the ones who will take the first swing at their brother or sister. Set up consequences before the act occurs.

Spend some time alone with each child. Do something that they like. Everyone has his or her own talents and interests. Take the time to bring these out in each child. Try not to make one child's interest more important than the others. Give each child a forum to air grievances. If your children know that there is a time and a place to air their grievances, they will use it. Try establishing a routine of discussing problems after dinner—over dessert makes it even better. Kids need to air their grievances with respect to their siblings, and you need to hear them out. No problem is too small.

 ESSENTIAL

> If one or both of your children have difficult personality traits such as extreme emotionality, negativity, or poor anger control, you will need to take extra steps to prevent abusive behavior between them.

Recognize cooperative behavior. If your children are able to work out a problem, take notice and give some praise. This will reinforce cooperation and help with future "battles."

A Child's Love Relationships

There are two specific times when your child can and does develop loving relationships without you. One is if there has been a breakup between the parents, and the other is when children grow up and begin to date.

Separation or Divorce

A divorce is the decision of the two people who were involved. It is not the decision of the children who have come from this marriage. How to handle parenting them after the decision to divorce is another separate decision.

When you divorce from your spouse, you are ending your loving relationship with him or her. You cannot, however, end the loving relationship between your child and your spouse. Their relationship needs to be respected. Children cannot simply turn off their emotions because adults might like them to. Your ex-spouse may be the biggest jerk in the world. It doesn't matter. Your child loves him or her. Your child needs to have the stability that comes from knowing that her parent still loves her. This stability will enable her to be resilient about the divorce.

 FACT

According to the National Census Bureau, the number of children living with both parents declined from 85 percent to 68 percent between 1970 and 1996. The proportion of children living with one parent has grown from 12 percent to 28 percent during this same time span.

Here are a few tips on how you can encourage the stability your child needs when there is a divorce in the family:

- Keep the lines of communication open.
- Keep your promises.
- Never talk negatively about your ex-spouse in front of your child.
- Do not talk about the legalities of the divorce in front of your children.
- Do not pump your child for information about your ex-spouse.
- Try to put differences aside and parent as a unit.
- Do not give in to the feeling that you need to one-up your ex-spouse if he or she gives a gift or something similar.
- Do not hold the court order over your child's head. If he wants to talk to your ex-spouse on a Tuesday, but that is your day, work it out and allow him.
- Enjoy the time with your child. Do not dwell on the bad feelings of divorce.

It is also important to uphold the relationships your child has in her life. She is her own person, with different relationships with the people who surround your family. Not only must you allow her to keep the relationships with grandparents, aunts, uncles, and others, you should promote them. Send a clear message that even though the family structure has changed, "family" is still important.

 QUESTION?

What if your spouse has done something wrong?
You should still never talk badly about your spouse in front of your child. When you do, your child will internalize it and wonder if she is bad also.

Tips for When Your Preteen Starts Dating

Another exciting time in your child's life is when he becomes interested in dating. You may have qualms about allowing him to date, but following these guidelines will help keep your child in age-appropriate activities and still allow him to enjoy the opposite sex.

- Do allow preteens to go out to places, i.e., roller-skating, school sporting events, and movies. Young teens like activities. Parents love it when they are active—it keeps them out of trouble.
- Do not allow them to go alone. At this age they do not need to have the conventional "date." Going out with their boyfriend/girlfriend with a group of friends is much more appropriate.
- Do allow them to invite their boyfriend/girlfriend over to your home. This is a great "set the stage" tip for later, when they become involved in more serious relationships. You will find if you make this a habit, you will be introduced to future dates without having to ask.

- Do not allow any inappropriate touching. Preteens are still children at heart and they will play games with the opposite sex (such as wrestling) that are no longer appropriate. Point these times out as they come along, without getting angry.
- Do give them the "talk" about sex. They need to know how their body is changing, and exactly what happens in the physical act of sex. Make sure the talk is not all straight facts. Give them your opinion on love and relationships.
- Do not give them permission to have sex. Just because you are letting them in on the facts about sex does not in any way mean you feel they are ready to engage in a sexual relationship.
- Do enjoy this time. Your child is growing up, and for all the awkwardness this issue can cause, it will be full of rewarding experiences.

When Your Teenager Starts Dating Seriously

Dating is one of the toughest topics for parents of older teenagers, because it leads to all the sex "stuff" that's out there, such as STDs, unwanted pregnancies, broken hearts, and so on. No one wants to deal with these topics, but as a parent you will need to. You need to set up a road map to follow when your teenager wants to start dating seriously on one-on-one dates.

Your goal as a parent is to be successful at helping your children accomplish the developmental goals of the teen years—reducing dependence on parents, while becoming increasingly responsible and independent. The key phrase to focus on here is *increasingly responsible and independent*. There is no age that is a "rite of passage" to a privilege. Dating is a privilege. All things with teenagers are situational and should be treated as such. Example: Your teenage daughter has been dating a nice boy for three months. You like him, so when she wants to go out on a car date, you allow it, saying, "Well, you're sixteen now, so I guess you're old enough." Two months down the road, they break up and she begins to see someone you really don't know very well.

She wants to go out with him on a car date, too. But now what do you say? She's still sixteen, and you don't have anything against this boy. But you're not as comfortable with it, are you?

When your son or daughter wants to start dating seriously, you need to set down your rules immediately. Here are a few suggestions:

- Never let your teenager out the door with anyone you haven't met—twice. This will ensure that you get to know whom your child is dating.
- Know where he is at all times. This is not your right as a parent; it's your responsibility.
- Set the curfew and the consequence before she is heading out the door for the date. It is easier to stick to a curfew if you don't have to come up with one on the spot.
- Treat his dates with respect and add a little humor.
- Give your teenager a backup plan should she need to get out of a bad situation that may arise on a date.

Problems to Look Out For

One of the biggest problems parents have when children begin dating is having the "sex talk" with them. This can be a scary time, and you need to have this talk with them long before you will feel they are ready to engage in this behavior.

While many teenagers wish they could talk to their parents about sex, most feel uncomfortable asking questions—and with good reason. It is very hard for parents not to jump to conclusions when these questions come up. But, please, don't assume that if your teenager asks questions about sex, she is necessarily thinking about having sex. If you don't give her information, she's going to get it from friends, television, and the movies, and much of what she learns may be wrong.

This is why it can be so important for us to keep the lines of communication open. Know what you're talking about. Times change, as have birth control methods and, unfortunately with the outbreak of AIDS, so have STDs. Learn what is out there today by doing your homework. Don't stop talking, and make sure you're listening to what they're saying, too. In order to get through the embarrassment you or your teenager may be having over the topic, bring it up often in general conversation. Ask his opinion when you see something on television or in the newspapers. Remember that conversation is a two-way street.

ESSENTIAL

Open communication is a must with your teenager when he begins dating. Share your dating stories with him to help give your conversations some give and take, not to mention some humor.

Fostering the Ability to Love

Love is a splendid thing. Giving or receiving love does not change with your child's development. You show your child love from the moment he is born through affection and by parenting him with all of the skills and tools you can muster. Your child loves you back, from the moment he is born, by showing you affection and, being your child, with all of the chocolate-face kisses, testing of limits, and everything else he does.

Enjoy being a loving family. Show affection even when you are angry. Talk and listen to each other. Respect and learn from each other. These are the things that will enable your child to someday love someone else too. Grandchildren are the ultimate fulfillment of teaching your child the ability to love. That is truly a success.

CHAPTER 22

Good Character

CREATING AN ENVIRONMENT in which your child can develop the habits of honesty, generosity, and a sense of justice is one of the hardest jobs of parenting. But these and many more good character traits will lead your child to success.

The Importance of Character

Your child needs to develop good character traits in order to gain respect and trust from those around him. When he has gained trust and respect from other people, including you, he will gain a sense of pride in his abilities that will boost his self-confidence.

The best way to teach character is by example. You can encourage character growth in your child by using, recognizing, requiring, and emphasizing right attitudes, words, and actions. Using the right attitudes, words, and actions is simple. You either model them, or you apologize for not modeling them.

Recognizing the right attitudes, words, and actions can be a little more difficult. It means you need to always be on the lookout for good behavior from your child. You are going to miss a few, to say the least. But do keep on the lookout. Praise your child out loud. You can also write him a note telling him how proud you are of how he handled a situation.

Requiring and emphasizing the right attitudes, words, and actions go hand in hand. Set your expectations for what is acceptable and what is not acceptable behavior beforehand by discussing the values of certain characteristics with the entire family. An easy way to do this is to discuss an aspect of good character weekly at the dinner table. Also, you can use teachable moments from television programs or books. You'll need to emphasize the character trait while your child is in a situation or after the situation has occurred. You can do this through praise or discipline.

Communicate Your Values Clearly

Clear communication of what good character traits you value is imperative. You need to communicate them with your words and actions. If you don't do as you say, you will give your child mixed messages.

Mixed messages are the angst of children whose parents talk to them about good character traits, and then exhibit the complete opposite behavior. You not only have to tell your children where you stand on an issue, you need to show them that you truly do feel that way by behaving as you said. For instance, if you don't want your children to smoke, then don't smoke. If you want your children to shake someone's hand when they meet or greet them, you should shake people's hands when you meet or greet them.

 ESSENTIAL

Clearly stating what you need from your child isn't always as easy as it sounds. Have your child repeat back what you said and what she thinks you meant. Then you can clear up any miscommunication.

Hold Your Child Accountable

When you set clear expectations, you need to hold your child accountable for her actions, each and every time. If her actions followed what you were expecting of her, then praise her. If her actions fell short of your expectations, then use the appropriate discipline. If you fail to be consistent and hold your child accountable, she will not learn the character trait you are trying to teach her.

Holding your child accountable does not, however, mean you should criticize her in front of other people, including in front of her friends. If you find your child is not being friendly, using good manners, or is being disrespectful, wait until you are alone with her before you point that out. If you discipline her immediately, the lesson you are trying to teach will be lost because your child will be too embarrassed to allow it to sink in.

Praising Character versus Praising an Action

As a parent you may get caught up in your child's actions, as opposed to the attitudes that produced his actions. This can get tricky if your child is in a competition of some sort. Say your child is an excellent speller, but he places fifth in a spelling bee. Does that make him any less of an excellent speller? No, it does not. Remember to praise his ability and his study skills, rather than being disappointed at the outcome of the competition.

 FACT

Praise good character out loud in front of other people, but never correct your child's character in front of other people. The first action will boost her self-esteem; the second action could totally destroy it.

Since your child's character determines his actions, it is more beneficial to praise his character rather than an action he took. For example, you should praise his good study skills rather than the high grade he received on a test. Let him know you appreciate it when he works hard at his schoolwork.

Personality Types and Character

A child's personality will lend itself to different aspects of good character. However, parents need to teach much of what makes their child have good character on a daily basis. Your child may also have a hard time with certain areas of good character because of her personality.

But whatever her personality type is, praise of good manners and respect is always warranted. Strive to recognize good character traits in your child at least three times a day. This helps with communication. Your child is more apt to tell you about her day when she is used to hearing praise about how she acted.

The Shy Child

If your child is shy, he may have a hard time with everyday manners. It may be hard for him to look a person in the eye when she is speaking. He may get nervous when he needs to say please or thank you. He may not speak up when he is treated unjustly. Or, he may have a hard time telling the truth if it will get someone else in trouble.

For this type of child, praise works best. First, acknowledge that you know he is trying and has a hard time. Tell him that being shy is okay and that you love him. Then, gently remind him of the character trait you are looking for and praise the little steps he has taken to achieve it.

Do not admonish the shy child when he is unable to comply. A shy child responds to praise well and will respond to negative talk by crawling deeper into his shell. Being somewhat shy is not a fault. But, if he thinks you feel he is less than perfect, you can drive him into being extremely shy, which will give him many problems as he grows.

The Overly Outgoing Child

The child who never stops going and is always waiting for the next thing to happen is the overly outgoing child. She can tend to run over people with her enthusiasm. She tends to talk a lot and be excited most of the time.

You will need to slow this child down. Remind her of manners and respect toward others in every teachable moment you can find. Praise her when she does use respect and use time-outs if you need to get her attention.

 ALERT!

When your overly outgoing child becomes a teenager, you may have to make him limit the activities he is involved in, just to make sure he doesn't overburden himself or leave himself with little downtime.

The Pleasing Child

The child who loves to please has some wonderful character traits. He has a happy attitude, he enjoys doing what he is asked, and he wants to make your day. He will go out of his way to do something nice for you. He makes friends easily and tends to keep them.

The problem this child has is that his good character is often taken advantage of. He has a hard time being honest about what he wants and will allow others to run all over him. Being true to yourself is also a good character trait and one that you will need to teach your pleasing child. How to say no firmly and respectfully is something he will need to learn.

Manners, Manners, Manners

Manners are everyday niceties that you will need to teach your child. They do not come naturally, although they are not hard to teach. Be consistent, use modeling, and explain to your child why you use a certain manner in a certain instance.

Saying Please and Thank You

How well do you model "please" and "thank you"? Do you use these polite words with your spouse? Do you use them with your children? Do you use them when you are angry? You need to use these words in your home every time they are appropriate; that includes with your spouse and child even if you are angry. It also includes the telemarketer who calls during dinner. Being polite—for example, "Please don't call here again. Thank you."—works very well with them, in fact. And you'll be modeling good manners to boot.

Start teaching manners to your child when she is very young. Even though an infant does not understand what you are saying, she knows you're saying something. As she grows, you will be pleased to hear her incorporate these words into her vocabulary. In fact, if you've started this right away, "please" and "thank you" will be among the first twenty words she says regularly.

There are a few times that your child may choose not to use these polite phrases. Sometimes it is on purpose and sometimes it is a mistake. For instance, when meeting someone who is a stranger, she may become very quiet and not speak. Some support and a gentle reminder will work here. Or, she may get angry with her siblings and not use her manners on purpose. You'll need to remind her that being angry is no excuse for being rude.

When your child is invited to do something with another family, remind her to always say "please" and "thank you." Simple reminders for everyday manners go a long way. Don't admonish her; just remind her. Your child is often just as busy as you are and with the excitement of going out with a friend, she may just simply forget.

Thank-You Notes

The art of sending thank-you notes may seem to be lost these days. The problem, in part, is the lack of organization by the parents and/or family. Your child will learn to write thank-you notes when you give him the ability to do so.

The easiest way to organize thank-you notes is to create a thank-you center. This could be either a folder or a basket. In your thank-you center you will need thank-you notes with envelopes, two pens or pencils, a list of phrase suggestions, and stamps. Make the list of phrase suggestions when you aren't already in the process of writing thank-you notes. Include simple phrases like:

"Thank you so much for . . . "
"I really enjoyed the . . . "
"I'm grateful you remembered my . . . "

Add to this list as you come up with new phrases. These phrases will help your child get started when she seems stumped or at a loss for how to begin.

Next, organize the timing. When holidays or birthdays approach, check your thank-you center supplies. As your child is opening gifts, have her list the gift and who gave it to her on a piece of paper. You'll have to do this for your younger child. The next day, sit down with your child and write out the thank-you notes.

One cute idea for children who are too young to write their names is to make a handprint, footprint, or fingerprint heart with a stamp pad. It will mean that you need to add a stamp pad (and some baby wipes for cleanup!) to your thank-you center. Simply put her selected body part on the stamp pad and then press it on the note. Fingerprint hearts are made by stamping your child's fingerprint twice—first in one diagonal direction and then in the other direction, with the top of the fingerprint forming the humps of the heart and the bottoms of the fingerprints meeting at a point. Three- to four-year-olds love doing these, as do school children. They tend to place it next to their name.

Other Manners

Miss Manners made a lifetime career out of the intricacies of manners. While it is impossible to list them all of them here, there are a few worth mentioning. When you teach your child these, family, friends, and strangers alike will look at him with respect.

First, never show disrespect with words or gestures, whether it is in front of someone or behind his or her back. Grunting, rolling the eyes, or any other disrespectful gesture is not allowed. There are more appropriate ways of showing your dissatisfaction and sometimes you just have to swallow it.

When your child coughs, burps, or sneezes, she should cover her mouth with her hand and say, "Excuse me." Not only is this polite, but it may keep her from spreading a cold or flu. Many school-age children think of these bodily functions as funny and they will laugh when they happen. To this age group, it is funny because these things sneak up on them. Gently remind them the proper way to handle the situation.

Second, teach your child always to look the person he is speaking to in the eye. To be preoccupied with something else when someone is speaking is rude. It is even ruder to totally ignore someone. Let your child know that this is inappropriate behavior.

Finally, teach your child to treat everyone with the same respect. Whether she likes someone does not gauge how she uses her manners. Someone else's behavior toward her does not give her the excuse to show disrespect in any way.

Sportsmanship and Being a Team Player

Sportsmanship and being a team player incorporate many different good character traits. Children are able to learn these great qualities easily when you get them involved in extracurricular activities that entail groups of their peers. Believe it or not, sportsmanship and being a team player do not necessarily have to involve a sport. Your child needs good sportsmanship when he plays checkers, too. He needs to be a team player to work on school projects in groups.

The first good character trait that sportsmanship and being a team player teaches children is how to be a hard worker. It shows them that to be good at something, you need practice, practice, and more practice! Your child will learn that when she works hard she becomes a valuable asset to her team. The next good character trait your child can learn is teamwork and cooperation. She will be able to see being on a team involves give-and-take. At times she will be the person taking, and at times she will need to give. She will learn that this is what makes a team work together to achieve its goal.

How to win gracefully and how to lose with dignity are also valuable lessons that sportsmanship and being a team player teaches. Rubbing a loss in a competitor's face is not acceptable behavior. While children get excited when they win, they always need to congratulate the other team for a game well played—even if it wasn't. When your child loses, she needs to learn to accept the loss and strive to do better next time. Do not allow her to make excuses or place blame on coaches or other team members. The fact is, sometimes the team wins, and sometimes it loses.

Coaches and youth organization leaders need to step up to the plate and be role models of the good characteristics that sportsmanship and being a team player can teach. If you find that your child's coach is not a decent role model, you may want to have a talk with her or the head of the league she is part of. Your child will become attached to this person and whether you like it or not she will have a big influence over your child's character.

Problems to Look Out For

One of the largest problems parents have when trying to teach good character is another person's child. When your child is interacting with a child who is behaving in a manner you think is unacceptable, you will sometimes feel the need to correct the child, even with the parent standing there. It is okay to do so if it is a simple correction of behavior, but do not cause a rift with the other parent over it.

If it becomes a larger problem, you will need to talk to the other parent about the situation. Explain what you are trying to do with your child and that you find it is not working when your children are together. Enlist the other parent's help instead of putting him or her on the defensive.

Activities That Foster Good Character

One of the best ways to foster good character is to attach a character trait to a goal your child has. When your child sees the value of the trait by seeing how it helps him obtain his goal, he will never forget the importance of that trait. Teach "please" and "thank you" right away by verbalizing it for young children. Before offering your child a cookie, say, "Please." After you hand it to her, say, "Thank you." Sharing and cooperation are also big lessons in character traits for toddlers. Praise him every step of the way when he shares a toy or a snack with you or a friend. Use discipline techniques should he take things from others. Teach him how to take turns by playing board games with him.

School-age children are capable of learning the more complicated good character traits such as sportsmanship, teamwork, and perseverance. At the dinner table, or during some one-on-one time, ask them, "What does it mean to be an honest/intelligent/caring person?" You may be surprised how much they already know. You can go further by asking, "Is it ever okay to be dishonest?"

Fables, virtue stories, and books are wonderful teaching tools for all kids. Spend some time reading these stories to your child, or have her read to you. Read the same books your teen is reading. Ask her what she thought the lesson was and if she agreed with the outcome. Discuss the traits the characters have.

Your teenager is going through the complicated time of finding his identity. He may test a few of his good character traits in order to do this. Constantly be on the lookout for when he does use his good character traits and praise him for it. Also, look for teachable moments when she tells you what went on in school. Ask your teenager how she would have handled a problem differently.

CHAPTER 23

Resilience

A CHILD CANNOT SUCCEED without resilience, the ability to face adversity and challenges with confidence. There has never been a day and age when this has been more important. From school stress to fights with friends, our children face adversity on a daily basis. Teach them how to have the confidence they need for a successful life.

Being Resilient

Children need to be able to bounce back from everyday dilemmas and challenges they encounter. They need to be able to solve problems. They need to be able to handle the mistakes they make. If they are unable to deal with these events, they will be unable to move on to the next predicaments, which are always right around the corner. In other words, they need to be resilient so they can face the challenges that life has in store for them and conquer them with confidence.

Resilience allows a child to cope with change. Changes happen every day in a child's life, such as having a substitute teacher in school, and they need to be able to handle them with little support from others. Most children have no problem because there is enough stability in their lives that a little change doesn't even make a blip on their radar. However, children who are going through big changes in their lives may have difficulty handling the little changes that occur.

Resilient children have a higher tolerance for frustration, better control of impulses, and more ability to delay gratification. While some children's personalities are more prone to these skills, all children can be taught them through good parenting. Resilient children become proficient in problem-solving because of these skills. Therefore, they are better able to confront challenges.

Learning as They Go

In order to solve problems and face challenges, children need to be able to put their frustrations aside and look at the whole picture instead of jumping in without thinking the second they see a problem. They need to delay their gratification and take their time to find the optimum solution. Stepping back from a problem can be very hard for children to do, and it definitely takes some practice.

 **FACT**

Project Competence is a study of 205 Minneapolis children that was initiated more than twenty years ago at the University of Minnesota. They found that children who succeeded in the face of adversity had more internal and external resources they could rely on, particularly in the form of good thinking skills and effective parenting.

Often children get stuck when working out challenges because they lack the experience of problem-solving. Therefore, they try the same solution over and over again, whether it works or not. They need a little help with their creativity in problem-solving. They need to look outside the box for other solutions that may help them.

You can help your child by slowing her down verbally when she seems stumped by a situation. Ask her to hold on a minute and think about what she really wants. Help her find different options to solving her problems by asking questions. Allow her to come up with solutions on her own but feel free to fine-tune them. By forcing your child to use her creativity in this way, you are teaching her to solve her own problems. You are showing her how to control her impulses and look for the best gratification.

Children who go through the motions of listing solutions to a problem, fine-tuning those solutions, and then choosing what solution they are going to try will learn resilience in real-time. This is to say, this method of overcoming a problem will become a habit. Since your child will face obstacles daily, his habit of solving them will become so quick that it may not seem as if he even went through all the motions. You will, however, be able to tell he is using this skill by his level of confidence when he is faced with a problem.

 ESSENTIAL

One of the hardest things to realize about parenting is to remember that you are always in the fish bowl. This can cause you some stress. Remember that no one is perfect and that you can always go back and fix it when you make a simple mistake like swearing.

Set a Good Example

When you face a problem, whether it is large or small, do you get frustrated or do you look forward to the challenge of solving it? Remember that children learn the most by observing how you handle situations. Resilience can be, and is, observed. Your child will learn to model your behavior when faced with similar challenges. So if you swear when you get stuck in traffic and voice out loud how terrible it is, complain that you will be late for your next appointment, the next time your child is held up and needs to wait, he will most likely not use patience. He may even repeat the phrases he heard you use and begin to rant.

You need to practice resilience, especially in front of your child, in order for him to be able to learn how to handle life's little frustrations. Train yourself to ask something like, "How should we handle this?" when faced with a frustrating situation. By verbalizing this in front of your child, you will show him how to go through the motions of solving the situation. He may even have some good ideas about what you should do.

Praise Your Child's Strengths

Children do not automatically know what they are good at. They do things and then wait for a reaction. If the reaction is positive and has value for them, they'll do it again. They'll keep doing it as long as they keep finding value in the action. Therefore, it follows that your child's strengths are in areas where she has found praise and value. Her strengths are where you have given her positive reinforcement.

Your child uses her strengths to face her challenges. She may succeed or she may fail. This can muddy the waters of what you should praise. You need to praise her strength and abilities, not the outcomes of her strengths and abilities. For example, say your ninth-grade daughter makes the junior varsity basketball team but has a problem with making foul shots. She just hasn't gotten the swing of them yet. So she spends time practicing every day. You go to her next game and she makes a foul shot. In order to praise her strength, you need to praise her fortitude in practicing for that shot, not just the fact that she made that one foul shot. Praise her strength in knowing how to face and overcome her challenge and she will be able to use it in many more areas of her life.

Accept Your Child's Personality

It is important to remember that we are all unique individuals who all have fingers but a completely different set of fingerprints. Your child is not an extension of you or your spouse.

He is his own person. When he is faced with a challenge, he may handle it differently than you would have. It may be the right way or it may be the wrong way. What is important to remember is that it is his way. Your child's personality comes through in his actions.

If your child is dramatic in nature and you are a shy person, you may not always appreciate the way he handles challenges. You may feel he makes too much of them. The way he handles things may not seem right to you. Learn to recognize that your child's personality is part of who he is, not just how he acts. By all means, offer options as solutions to his challenges that reflect your personality, but accept that he is the one who has the choice. Accept that his personality is as unique as your own.

Use Your Parenting Skills and Tools

In order to encourage resilience in your child, you will need to use all of your parenting skills and tools. They all offer a piece of what your child needs to become someone who can successfully handle adversity. Although this may sound as though you will have to be perfect all of the time, that really isn't so.

The most important tool is modeling your own decision-making skills. Open communication becomes important when you are helping your child list solutions to a problem. Remember to use door openers instead of door slammers. Give each of your children some of your time. One-on-one time helps open the lines of communication. Use your emotional intelligence and listen with an empathetic but reasonable ear. Offer suggestions but don't solve your child's problems for her.

Revise, Renew, and Reconsider Rules Often

Are you comfortable setting a limit for your child and not checking every minute whether she is within your limit? Do you communicate your expectations clearly to your child and then take out the spyglass to watch whether he meets that expectation? Or do you not even set limits and expectations, and simply hold your child's hand through every task?

With every stage of your child's development, rules should be updated. You do not have to tell your five-year-old not to climb up on the table as you did when she was a toddler. You do not have to walk your fifteen-year-old across the street. Most of the limits and expectations you set for your child will need to change over time.

You will need to let go of your control with each step of your child's development. Have your child be involved in the making and changing of rules by asking her what privileges she would like to have and what responsibilities she feels she can handle. By renewing your rules often, you are allowing your child room to grow.

Overcoming Common Obstacles

Resilient children learn to overcome everyday obstacles by not fearing failure. Mistakes are not something to be afraid of; they only give you a chance to try again. Think of it this way: People need to make mistakes to learn. If mistakes are thought of as learning tools, and not something to be ashamed of, there is no reason to fear them.

 ESSENTIAL

Remember to use your parenting tools: discipline, communication, modeling, family traditions and rituals, and problem-solving. They are the backbone of your actions as a parent. Using these with your natural parenting skills will help your child learn to be resilient.

You can help your child not become afraid of making mistakes by using your communication tools. First and foremost, your parenting tone needs to remain even and calm when your child makes a mistake. This is easier said than done when your four-year-old spills milk down the inside of your refrigerator and you're wondering why she was in there in the first place. Or your nine-year-old son has taken to riding his bike in the street and has somehow forgotten to look both ways when he crosses an intersection. Deep breaths and count backward from ten . . . or from one hundred.

Second, use I-messages to help your child label how she is feeling. "I understand that you are frustrated, but you may not jump off of the table." When your child labels her feelings, she can comprehend and control them better. She will be able to delay her impulses long enough to find a solution.

Last, but not least, use your active listening skills. In order for you to offer your child options as solutions, you need to understand the problem she is facing. You need to hear her. She needs your undivided attention. Ask her questions about what you don't understand and listen to her answers. When you feel you understand the problem, then offer solutions.

There are times when you should not help your child with a problem. For instance, if your child simply doesn't want to face the challenge but needs to. In this instance, you need to allow your child to fail. Once he does, do not allow him to blame other people or external circumstances for his failure. Offer him solutions on how he can change the outcome the next time he faces a similar challenge. Support him by saying you know he is capable of succeeding and that you hope the next time he will try harder.

Overcoming Hard-Hitting Obstacles

Unfortunately, there are problems that can happen that no parent wants their child to face. But since you can't always prevent the challenges, you want to be sure your child is able to face the situations with the tools to get through. Resilient children are capable of facing these challenges and still, given time, live life with confidence in their abilities. They are able to bounce back from their trauma and still relate competently to others. They are able to succeed.

Of course, it takes time. Overcoming hard-hitting obstacles isn't like trying to complete a homework assignment. There are normal stages everyone needs to go through when faced with a life-altering trauma or a loss: denial, anger, bargaining, depression, and finally, acceptance. Resilient children are able to go through each of these stages and come out with strength of character and confidence in their abilities.

ALERT!

Teenagers who are going through rough times because of hard-hitting obstacles tend to act out using risk-taking behaviors. They may seek out drugs to escape their problems. If this is your child, get her some professional help.

Problems to Look Out For

There are a couple of reasons a child may begin to experience stress when faced with a challenge or obstacle. Sometimes this stress is evident in acting out behaviors or physical problems. If your child exhibits physical signs of stress, have him see the doctor immediately. Some common signs of stress include:

- Withdrawal
- Fatigue
- Muscle tremors
- Vomiting
- Grinding of the teeth
- Blackouts
- Headache
- Shortness of breath

Trying and Failing . . . and Failing Again

While your child needs to be able to bounce back from her mistakes, she is not made of rubber. Failing more than once or twice when faced with the same challenge may make your child give up. When you see this happening, check to see if the challenge is above her developmental level. If it is, offer loving support or alternative solutions. If it isn't, help her through it. For instance, a three-year-old may be able to get his shorts on but have a hard time putting on his socks because his fine motor skills aren't ready yet. There is absolutely nothing wrong with a little help here and there. After all, what are parents for?

 FACT

Under stress, the body produces an increase in the hormones adrenaline, noradrenaline, and corticosteroids. In the short-term, these hormones produce tense muscles, queasiness, and an increase in breathing and heart rate. Long-term complaints that are stress related include high blood pressure and heart disease.

The Big Things and the Little Things

When big changes happen or huge challenges come your child's way, he may be able to handle them with ease. Then all of a sudden, he becomes stressed out over the simplest thing. This is because there is only so much a child, or an adult, can take. Even the most resilient child will need to take a break from handling challenges now and again. This is especially important when he is not capable of controlling what is going on. For instance, when there is a death in the family. While your child is upset and sad, he seems to go on just like everyone else. But then, *wham!* He socks his brother in the face for taking his radio; something he would have never done before, and you're shocked. Experts term this *acting out behavior.*

While acting out behavior can't be condoned, it is under-standable, even for the most resilient child. When this happens, you'll need to be understanding of the situation, but firm in the discipline for the action. Explain to your child that while you understand that strong feelings can lead him to do things that he wouldn't normally do, there are still consequences for actions such as punching his brother. Then follow through with your normal discipline.

The Battering Ram

While there will be many wonderful teachers and people who have authority over your children, there will be some who aren't as wonderful. When your child is dealing with a teacher who is hard on them, uses negative talk, fails to praise when appro-priate, she is actually juggling three different challenges: (1) to learn the lesson she is there for, (2) to deal with the teacher in an appropriate way, and (3) to ward off the battering ram to her self-esteem.

 ALERT!

Do not assume a teacher is being overly hard on your child or too negative every time your child has a problem. If you are concerned, call and speak with your child's teacher or set up an appointment.

This may show up in her grades in that subject and attitude about the class. Know that your child is capable of handling diffi-cult people in her life—she needs to learn that lesson, too—and offer her support by going through the options and listing solutions for dealing with her teacher. Give her some extra help with her les-sons and, most important, praise her even more.

Activities That Foster Resilience

Teach your child to be resilient by using everyday challenges. Allow him time to adapt to changes and give him support and an empathetic ear when needed. Praise his abilities and strengths often.

Activities for Babies and Toddlers

Babies have to adapt to change quite a bit, since everything is new to them. Soothing words, rocking, and holding them will make them feel secure when adjusting to changes. Provide unconditional love both verbally and nonverbally.

As your child grows, help her begin to accept responsibility for her own behavior and to understand that her actions have consequences. Gradually expose your child to challenging situations in books and explain what the character did to solve the problem.

 FACT

When they are toddlers, resilient children display an array of characteristics. Intelligence, autonomy, and sociability are present during the toddler years. Their autonomy is tempered by adequate cooperation and compliance. They are friendly, socially responsive, and sensitive, with a positive sense of self.

Activities for School-Age Children

Encourage this age group to use problem-solving skills by modeling them. Use books and television programs to practice "What would you do?" situations. This age group loves puzzles and riddles, which sharpen their problem-solving skills.

School-age children also begin to develop true friendships. With these new relationships comes a quarrel or two with their friends. Help them sort out their feelings and list their options for dealing with quarrels. Give them the pros and cons for each option but allow them to choose their own solution.

Activities for Teens

There is a misconception among parents that when their child reaches the teenage years, it is time to let her solve her own problems. Although teens may want some extra space to demonstrate their independence, this statement couldn't be further from the truth. They still need someone to bounce ideas off of and to have an empathetic ear.

This age group is still into puzzles, especially logic puzzles, and they enjoy a good mystery. Many of their problem-solving abilities are formed, and you can enjoy watching them think things through. There will be times, however, when you will be wondering what they were thinking. This is because teenagers tend to be risk takers, and therefore, their decisions aren't always the best.

CHAPTER 24

Saving the Best for Last

I N THE END, you hope that all of your hard work pays off. Your child will go on to have a happy, productive, and successful life. You will have the pride of a job well done. Better yet, you may even get grandchildren!

How Do You Know if It Worked?

There is a feeling that will come over you when you realize that your child is not a child anymore. You'll walk into his home, have dinner at his table, and you'll know. It isn't like fireworks going off, and there won't be a neon sign above his head blinking *I'm all grown up now!* It will be a comfortable feeling that everything is right and the way it should be.

By teaching your child the attributes for success, you'll see him strive for success in all areas of his life. You'll know that he learned the ability to love by the way he loves someone special in his life. You'll know he has a willingness to learn by the way he seeks out interesting topics. You'll know that he is resilient by the way he handles challenges. You'll know he has a high self-esteem and good character by his actions toward other people and toward himself. You'll know when something is wrong because of the relationship you have built with him throughout his childhood.

ESSENTIAL

Communication is just as important, if not more important, when your child is an adult as when she was school-age. While you may need to accept more independence from your child, you still have the responsibility of voicing your opinion and feelings.

Giving Up Control

One of the hardest jobs parents have to face is giving up more and more control as a child gets older. How much do you allow her to do? Will she want more? What happens if you give her too much control?

As with all the lessons you will teach your child, this one has rules that are not set in stone. You'll need to take a look at where your child is at in taking responsibility for her actions. You can choose to give in some areas and not in others. Start by asking your teenager what she feels she can handle. Is there an area where she is feeling controlled and she would like to do more independently? Your child will take more responsibility if the area in which she is taking more control was the area she wanted in the first place.

Adult Children at Home

Whether your child chooses to attend college, a technical school, or start working after high school, he will need a place to live when he gets started. That place may be home with you. Or he may need a home base to visit when the school shuts down for holiday or summer vacations. You'll need to set your expectations with him on the limits and rules before he is off and running.

The biggest complaint parents have at this time is the use of their house as though it is an apartment. Adult children often come and go without respect for the others that live in the home. Of course, your adult child wants to be independent. But the fact is, she isn't independent if she is still living with you. So, some consensus needs to be reached. Discuss what your expectations are going to be, and don't call them your child's rules, call them the house rules. For example, curfews tend to make adult children antsy. But you can explain that when someone comes into the house after three in the morning, you wake up, and it's disturbing. Therefore, if she is going to be out past midnight, you would like her to call you to let you know.

Empty Nest

The transition between being a parent of a teenager and a parent of an adult child is yet another difficult time for parents. It can be heartbreaking and heartwarming at the same time. Know that with all you have done with parenting, you are capable of this too. There are a few things that you can do to help you through this time.

 ESSENTIAL

Make those care packages. You can still do things for your child, and it will make you feel better to do them. There is nothing better than getting groceries from Mom, or a set of towels for the new apartment. Try not to overdo in the beginning, and don't add any strings to the gifts.

Do something new or different! Volunteer, take a class, find a new hobby, or pick up an old one. Anything that will take up the time you devoted to your teenager on a daily basis. Take a trip and take your honey. Rekindle your romance by taking off somewhere, talking about the future, and making plans. Think of it as a second honeymoon that will start off the second part of your relationship. Many parents report that the love affair with their spouse after the children have left the nest is better than the one that produced them.

Make use of the space in your home. Although you don't want to make your child feel like you're pushing him out the door, make plans for the space that he has occupied before he leaves. Order something new for the room that will come in a couple of days after he leaves. If you wait until he's really gone, you may find yourself putting it off.

Congratulate yourself and get support if you need it. Although the job of being a parent is never done, you have reached a goal. You have raised an independent young adult, which is no easy task. Give yourself a pat on the back for a job well done. If you find you are having a very hard time with your child leaving home, get some help from your family doctor, clergy, or other parents. Life changes are extremely hard, and the empty nest syndrome can make the postpartum blues look like a skip through the meadow.

Looking Back

Part of how you know you were successful in parenting your child is if you can look back and know that you and your child enjoyed the journey. When your child is home for the holidays, does she laugh as you regale her about past holiday seasons? Do her old school pictures bring a smile to your face?

Take a look back and remember the times you enjoyed traveling the road of parenthood. Write them down in a journal, now that you have the time. Keep these successes handy to use to entertain your grandchildren.

Creating Your Own Luck

Parents create their own luck. By learning to use their parenting skills, they form their child's attributes that make parenting easier. As you develop more skills and make them unique to your family, you'll feel like one lucky parent of an obedient child.

There is a learning curve, for both you and your child. When you learn a new skill, you will be more uncomfortable with it after using it once or twice. After the third time, however, there is an upswing, and by the tenth time, it will be second nature. Your child will do the same as you try out your new skill or parenting tool on him. If you use it consistently, they will begin to respond positively. Then, they will make you look like one of those lucky parents with well-brought-up children.

 ALERT!

A parent who is counting on luck with his or her children has not developed a sense of resilience. While things happen that are out of your control, you do have the ability to face those challenges.

Congrats on Your Successful Child

The vast majority of parents just want their child to be happy and healthy. Successful children are. They are also able to talk honestly with their parents, enjoy being loved and loving back, enrich themselves, feel good about who they are, and be respected by others. Whether they attend college or have a family will be a choice they will have to make. You have given them the opportunity to choose wisely by using all your parenting abilities, and through some blood, sweat, and tears.

As you continue on your journey of parenting, enjoy your child. Set your goals together and develop as individuals. Their success, and yours, will come from one infallible fact—you love them.

APPENDIX A
Book Resources

10-Minute Life Lessons for Kids: 52 Fun and Simple Games and Activities to Teach Your Child Honesty, Trust, Love, and Other Important Values
By Jamie C. Miller
Perennial, October 1998

20 Teachable Virtues: Practical Ways to Pass on Lessons of Virtue and Character to Your Children
By Barbara C. Unell, Jerry L. Wyckoff (Editor)
Perigee, August 1995

365 Manners Kids Should Know: Games, Activities, and Other Fun Ways to Help Children Learn Etiquette
By Sheryl Eberly
Three Rivers Press, November 2001

365 Positive Strategies for Single Parenting
By Susan B. Brown, Monica Simmons
Smyth & Helwys Pub, April 1998

American Academy of Pediatrics Guide to Your Child's Symptoms
By Donald Schiff (Editor), Steven P. Shelov (Editor), American Academy of Pediatrics
Villard, January 1997

Bringing Out the Best in Your Child: 80 Ways to Focus on Every Kid's Strengths
By Cynthia Ulrich Tobias, Carol Funk (Contributor)
Servant Publications, February 1997

Discover Your Child's Learning Style
By Mariaemma Willis, Victoria Kindle-Hodson
Prima Lifestyles, October 1999

Emotional Intelligence
By Daniel Goleman
Bantam, July 1997

The Family Virtues Guide: Simple Ways to Bring Out the Best in Our Children and Ourselves
By Linda Kavelin Popov, Dan Popov (Contributor), John Kavelin (Contributor)
Plume, June 1997

Grandparenting with Love & Logic: Practical Solutions to Today's Grandparenting Challenges
By Jim Fay
Love & Logic Press, September 1998

Growing Up Again: Parenting Ourselves, Parenting Our Children
By Connie Dawson, Jean Illsley Clarke
Hazelden Information Education, May 1998

Growing Up Confident: How to Make Your Child's Early Years Learning Years
By Melitta J. Cutright
Doubleday, February 1992

How to Talk so Kids Will Listen and Listen so Kids Will Talk
By Adele Faber, Elaine Mazlish
Avon, October 1999

Kids Can Cooperate: A Practical Guide to Teaching Problem Solving
By Elizabeth Crary
Parenting Press, March 1984

Love and Anger: The Parental Dilemma
By Nancy Samalin, Catherine Whitney
Penguin USA, July 1995

Love & Limits: Achieving a Balance in Parenting
By Ronald Huxley
Singular Publishing, July 1998

Parenting with Love and Logic: Teaching Children Responsibility
By Foster W. Cline, Jim Fay
Navpress, October 1990

P. E. T.: Parent Effectiveness Training
By Thomas Gordon
Three Rivers Press, October 2000

Pick Up Your Socks . . . and Other Skills Growing Children Need!
By Elizabeth Crary, Pati Casebolt (Illustrator)
Parenting Press, March 1990

Positive Discipline for Single Parents: Nurturing, Cooperation, Respect and Joy in Your Single-Parent Family
By Jane Nelsen, Cheryl Erwin, Carol Delzer
Prima Lifestyles, October 1999

Positive Self-Talk for Children
By Douglas Bloch, Jon Merritt (Contributor)
Bantam, December 1993

Protecting the Gift: Keeping Children and Teenagers Safe (And Parents Sane)
By Gavin De Becker
Dell, May 2000

Raising Emotionally Intelligent Teenagers
By Maurice J. Elias, Steven E. Tobias, Brian S. Friedlander
Harmony Books, September 2000

Raising Respectful Kids in a Rude World
By Gary D. McKay, Joyce L. McKay, Steven Maybell, Daniel Eckstein
Prima Lifestyles, April 2001

Siblings Without Rivalry: How to Help Your Children Live Together So You Can Live Too
By Adele Faber, Elaine Mazlish
Avon, February 1998

So You Want to Be a Stay-At-Home Mom
By Cheryl Gochnauer
Intervarsity Press, August 1999

What to Expect When You're Expecting
By Heidi E. Murkoff, Arlene Eisenberg, Sandee Hathaway
Workman Publishing Company, April 2002

APPENDIX B
Web Resources

AARP: Grandparents Raising
Grandchildren
www.aarp.org

Adoption
http://adoption.about.com

American Academy of
Pediatrics
www.aap.org

Children's Books
*http://childrensbooks.
about.com*

ChildStats.gov
www.childstats.gov

Commonsense Parenting
www.parenting.org

Disney's Family.com
http://family.go.com

Divorce and Single Parenting
www.divorcewizards.com

Family Crafts
http://familycrafts.about.com

Family Education Network
www.familyeducation.com

Family First Aid
www.familyfirstaid.co.uk

Family Internet
*http://familyinternet.
about.com*

Fatherhood
http://fatherhood.about.com

Homemaker Magazine
www.homemaker.uk.net

InnerSelf Magazine: Parenting
www.innerself.com

Inspirational Mail: Family Life
www.inspirationalmail.com

KidSource Online
www.kidsource.com

Kids' Turn Central
www.kidsturncentral.com

Movie Mom's Reviews
*http://movies.yahoo.com/
moviemom*

National Education Association
www.nea.org

National Parent Information
Network
✍ *http://npin.org*

National PTA
✍ *www.pta.org*

The National Parenting Center
✍ *www.tnpc.com*

The New Homemaker
✍ *www.newhomemaker.com*

Nibbles . . . Ideas for Family
✍ *www.urbanext.uiuc.edu/
nibbles*

Pampers Parenting Institute
✍ *www.pampers.com*

Parental Media Guide
✍ *www.parentalguide.org*

Parenting of Adolescents
✍ *http://parentingteens.
about.com*

Parenting Babies and Toddlers
✍ *http://babyparenting.
about.com*

Parenting of K–6 Children
✍ *http://childparenting.
about.com*

Parenting of Multiples
✍ *http://multiples.about.com*

Parenting Special Needs
✍ *http://specialchildren.
about.com*

Parenting.com
✍ *www.parenting.com*

ParentingHumor.com
✍ *www.parentinghumor.com*

Parentstages.com
✍ *www.parentstages.com*

Positive Parenting
✍ *www.positiveparenting.com*

Pregnancy and Birth
✍ *http://pregnancy.about.com*

PrimeTap: Family and Home
✍ *http://primetap.com/
fhome.html*

Simply Family Magazine
✍ *www.simplyfamily.com*

Single Parents
✍ *http://singleparents.
about.com*

SingleParentsMag.com
✍ *www.singleparentsmag.com*

Stay-at-Home Parents
✐*http://homeparents.*
about.com

Stepfamily Foundation
✐*www.stepfamily.org*

The Successful Parent
✐*www.thesuccessful*
parent.com

Teen Moms Club
✐*www.teenmomsclub.com*

The WholeFamily Center
✐*www.wholefamily.com*

Index

WE HAVE EVERYTHING

FOR PARENTING!

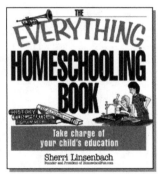